GW00385341

On My Toes

Maureen Smith

With a Foreword
by
Group-Captain Douglas Bader
C.B.E., D.S.O., D.F.C.

FREDERICK MULLER

First published in Great Britain in 1972 by
Frederick Muller Limited, Ludgate House, 110 Fleet Street,
London EC4A 2AP

Printed by Northumberland Press Ltd., Gateshead.
Bound by Garden City Press, Letchworth.

SBN: 584 10193 7

Contents

Contents

Foreword

by Group-Captain Douglas Bader

C.B.E., D.S.O., D.F.C.

Books written about people who are different, whether like this one they be autobiographies or biographies written by someone else, fascinate me.

Maureen Smith has decided to write her own story and here it is. It is a factual account of a girl who was born with only one sound limb – a leg. She arrived in this world without arms and with one leg twisted and feeble.

To start life with such a physical disadvantage would seem to be a daunting prospect to those of us who have been lucky enough to be born whole.

The narrative is simply written and provides a faithful record of how Maureen, with the aid and affection of her equally courageous parents, has managed to lead a comparatively normal life for the last twenty-seven years. It contains no false heroics – there is no need, the facts speak for themselves.

One line from this book stays in my mind because of its absolute truth: "Independence of any kind is most important to a disabled person."

14th July 1972

I
The Family

It was a hot sunny afternoon in the Norfolk village of Gayton when I made my entrance into the world on August 1st,
1943. My parents had no idea that the daughter they so
dearly wished for would be different in any way from
any other child, simply because nobody knew.

Our home was a normal, happy home, one of a pair of
small farm cottages in a village in the heart of war-time
Norfolk. It was no picturesque, thatched cottage, but a
solid building of red brick built near the turn of the
century. There were only two bedrooms and one downstairs room and none of the modern conveniences that
have in recent years made life a little easier for the hard-
working farm labourer.

In the olden days farm workers were mainly illiterate
men but this has long ceased to be so. With the coming
of machinery it has become necessary not only to be able
to use these beasts of steel, but to know how to keep them
in good working order. And yet farm labourers are still
amongst the lowest paid workers in the country.

My father, Charles, who for some unknown reason was
called Jack, was an introvert who enjoyed his Sunday
lunch-time pint at the local. He was wiry with very dark
hair and the ruddy complexion that is common to people

who lead an open-air life. He worked long hours as a tractor driver and then spent the evenings happily working in the garden growing vegetables, and tending the pigs and poultry he used to keep for the extra meat and eggs which helped out in those days of ration books. Farm-workers were exempt from call-up but he joined the men of the Home Guard who were ready to protect the British Isles from invasion. A Section was lucky to be issued with even one rifle and often there was no ammunition supplied with it. However the men rarely lost heart and managed by using such things as sticks and pitchforks as weapons.

My mother, Maud, had worked at a local grocery store before her marriage and for some of the War years she continued by driving a van on a paraffin delivery round. She was a dark-haired, plump, home-loving person who was very fond of children. She was contented looking after her home, sewing, reading her weekly magazine and visiting her parents and the members of her family who lived in the village. One of her sisters, Queenie, lived in the next cottage to ours and was expecting her first baby only a few weeks after I was due to be born.

I had a brother, Bernard, who was four and a half years my senior. He was a fair, curly haired, shy child who had a mania for burying his toys in the garden and saying they were people in the village he did not like. He was a premature baby; though seeing him now it is difficult to believe! He has grown into a well-built, good-looking young man, and although his hair darkened it remained wavy. He gradually lost much of his former shyness and gained confidence in himself.

My father's parents had both died, his mother when he was only five years old and his father some twenty years later. But my mother's parents lived nearby and so we saw them often. They were wonderful grandparents and we were very fond of them. I cannot remember my grandfather very clearly, but I do recall vividly how I liked sitting on a cushion on my Granny's kitchen table. This was probably because I could see better from there what was happening around me: I never liked to miss anything.

My mother was the eldest of a family of nine; my father was one of three children and he also had four step-brothers and sisters as his father had married again. Therefore my family was completed by numerous aunts and uncles, and an ever-increasing number of cousins.

Even back in 1943 Gayton was a large village but in the last ten years its boundaries have spread further, rather like the tentacles of an octopus. This expansion in villages has been caused by the population explosion which occurred immediately after the war. There were four public houses in Gayton (two are now closed), two butcher's shops, three general stores, Post Office, a fourteenth-century church and a chapel. Our house was situated beside the main road, only a few yards from the primary school. An alley-way separated the back of the houses from the churchyard. Nearly all of the menfolk worked on farms as there was no other work in the village, and very few factories at that time in the nearby market town of King's Lynn.

Dances were held in Gayton but the nearest cinema was in King's Lynn. The big event of the year in the area was the visit of the well-known Mart, this was a fun-fair which opened on St Valentine's Day and stayed for ten days (this event still takes place). Our parents always took Bernard and me when we were children, and although I enjoyed watching I never longed to have a ride on the various roundabouts; I much preferred our annual visit to the pantomime.

During the hot summer months of 1943 the Smiths made the arrangements for the birth of their second child. Bernard was to stay with his grandparents and Aunt Edith who would be on holiday from her job in London, so there would be plenty of people to look after him. It was arranged for a woman to look after things at home; a neighbour, Mrs Goodbody, was to assist Nurse Grimes (the district nurse) at the actual birth. If she needed him the nurse could always contact the local G.P., Dr Devlin, a blunt but kindly Irishman. So all the preparations were completed for the arrival of the baby.

When I was born on that Sunday afternoon neither Nurse Grimes nor Mrs Goodbody gave any sign that things were not normal. For that my mother always admired them. Mrs Goodbody did leave the bedroom soon after my birth, but she was getting on in years and so my mother did not think there was anything strange about her going downstairs. After she was settled comfortably my mother asked what her baby was, a boy or girl.

When Nurse told her a girl she replied, "Why ever didn't you tell me? You knew I wanted a girl this time."

There was much discussion downstairs as to who was to break the news to my mother that her baby was deformed. My father tried but obviously he did not succeed as my mother thought he meant that my arms were twisted.

She said, "Well they can do such wonderful things these days." When she did understand that I had no arms at all she kept asking, "Well where are they then?" It was some days later before she learned that my left leg also was not normal.

My grandparents and aunt brought Bernard home after tea to see his sister. When my mother started to explain that he must be gentle with the new baby my aunt said, "We have already told him."

My mother learnt afterwards that Bernard had eaten very little of his tea that day. This was not because he was upset by the news but simply because he was so excited at having a sister!

During the first week my aunts and uncles from Cambridge and Yorkshire came as soon as they heard the news, and Aunt Edith took an extended holiday. Nothing like it had happened previously in the family and therefore it was difficult for them to believe. They could not even remember hearing about such a case before. But as my grandfather commented, "If you read about anything like this in the newspapers you take no notice, it means nothing until it happens to you."

Although I was otherwise a perfectly healthy baby my mother wanted me christened as soon as possible, as she did wonder at first if I would live. I was named Maureen Betty at the ceremony which was performed at home when I was a few days old. Some months later I was received into the church at the same time as my cousin, Betty, was christened.

My disability was, of course, an enormous shock to my parents and they could not imagine me being able to move around or do anything for myself at all. Dr Devlin and Nurse Grimes were very kind and kept assuring them that things would turn out better than they seemed to be at present. But as neither of them knew personally of a similar case their reassurances could not have been really convincing.

When I was five weeks old I made the first of several visits to the world famous Great Ormond Street Hospital for Sick Children in London, where I was seen by Mr Denis Browne, September 13th, 1943, who always called me his "little friend from Norfolk".

On that first visit I had numerous X-rays and tests. I expressed my disapproval of the whole procedure by struggling violently when they tried to hold me still for the X-rays. The doctors, however, could not explain why the deformities had occurred: growth had just stopped. They were all kind but there was nothing they could actually do. So home I went.

2
Early Months

When my parents had recovered from the initial shock of
my disability they made plans for the future. It was obvious
that I should need a great deal of care and attention, but
they resolved right from the beginning to treat me as
normally as possible. My mother said she would dress me
in pretty clothes and anything that I wanted, within reason,
I was to have, but at the same time they agreed not to
spoil me.

I rewarded my mother's loving care by being a far from
good baby. She spent many nights sitting up in bed with
me in her arms, she was so afraid I would wake Bernard
with my crying. My distress was probably due to the fact
that I have always suffered considerably from indigestion:
well that is my excuse and I am sticking to it! There must
be some truth in my theory though, as my mother eventually
discovered something which helped to soothe me, it was a
little brandy mixed with warm water and sugar.

Lord Romney was the owner of the farms in Gayton,
he lived with his wife at Gayton Hall. After they heard
about me Lady Romney wrote to my mother asking if
she could come to see her.

When Lady Romney, a tall and graceful woman then in
middle age, duly arrived, she said, "I have come to ask

you something, but it is difficult to know how to put it, I do hope you won't be offended. Would you rather have Maureen put into a home?"

My mother exclaimed, "No, we intend to manage to look after her ourselves."

Lady Romney said, "I only asked because I could have probably helped if it had been what you wanted, I won't mention it again."

The subject was never raised again but Lady Romney continued to take a close interest in my progress. It was through her that Lady Cynthia Colville designed some clothes for me.

My mother thought I would look better in a cape rather than a matinee jacket with sleeves and so she wrote to Patons & Baldwin asking them if they would make up a cape pattern. They not only sent a pattern but the girls there had knitted a blue cape and also made a pair of padded arms to match.

I had cut my first two teeth by the time I was six months old. Shortly after that I began to play with the rattle that was on the side of my pram by using my right foot. Also I started to grip people's fingers with my toes as other babies do with their fingers. At first I only used my right foot so obviously I was going to be "right-handed".

I would lie in my pram with my foot on the side of it displaying all my frills. People said what a lovely baby I was in my dainty outfits and with my thick chestnut hair (which had been black at birth). I never liked the hot sun when I was a child and in summer months my hair would cling to my head in little damp curls.

I was not allowed to sit up at too early an age as my mother was afraid the strain on my back would be too great. But after I had reached this stage I made attempts to feed myself. I would hold a biscuit with my left foot and by bending forward I could reach my mouth. Gradually I progressed to using a spoon and fork with my right foot and also I could manage a cup by putting my big toe through the handle. Although these were only small things they brought a glimmer of hope for the future to my parents, who always encouraged me in each new achievement.

The only setbacks I had was when I cut any teeth and then I always had bronchitis. As well as being a worry to my family it was also costly as in those days there were still doctor's fees to pay. On one occasion I developed pneumonia and I was so poorly that one doctor told my parents that he doubted if I would survive. But Dr Devlin said more reassuringly, "Where there's life there's hope," and thanks to my family's devoted care I recovered.

My mother would often sit me on the hearthrug while she did her household chores. She clearly remembers doing this one day, in particular, when I was about fourteen months old. She was ironing and when she looked to see what I was doing I was over near the back door. She could not imagine how I had crossed the floor as I had never previously moved unaided. It was several days before I repeated the performance but I was soon crawling around the house like lightning on my bottom. So much so that during the summer months when the back door was open there had to be a board across the bottom of the opening to stop me getting outside.

In February 1945 my family read in the local newspaper of the death of an artist, Ted Gosling, who was also armless. He was a native of Heacham, a small seaside resort on the North Norfolk coast; he lived in Manchester for several years and it was there that he had met his wife. However, after their marriage they had made their home in North Wales.

My mother wrote to Mrs Gosling telling her about me. She received a reply at first from the Matron of a Children's Home near Old Colwyn where Mr Gosling had been Secretary. Later there was a letter from Mrs Gosling herself, in which she mentioned that she had planned to visit Heacham that summer with her husband. My mother said in her reply that we lived quite near to Heacham so if Mrs Gosling would still like to make her visit to Norfolk she would be very welcome to stay with us. She added that we were only an ordinary working-class family.

Mrs Gosling arrived in time for my second birthday celebrations and she has visited us regularly ever since. She immediately seemed like one of the family. To Bernard and I she has always been known as "Aunt" Rene. It was a great encouragement to my parents hearing about the active life Mr Gosling had led. As well as being an artist he was also good at woodwork, one of the last things he made was a horse on wheels and Aunt Rene gave this to me.

Bernard had a beautiful white cat for a pet: it was killed some years later by a lorry. So my parents decided to give me a dog, she was only a bundle of black fur with a white splash on her chest when she came. I was sitting on the hearthrug when the man brought her, he put her down on the floor just inside the door and she walked straight over to me. Wendy, as we called her, was never boisterous with me. In the summer she would walk miles with Aunt Rene and I when we went blackberrying and she never had to wear a lead. Although she was not the thoroughbred she should have been she was a wonderful companion, almost human. In later years when we were getting ready to go out Wendy, without being told, would go over to her shed (we never closed the door) and when we arrived home she would be waiting at the gate to greet us. It was a great loss when she died on Bernard's twenty-first birthday.

As the months passed by I began doing more and more with my feet. I played the usual children's games with my cousins who lived next door, Betty and I would play happily together but when her younger sisters, June and Christine, joined us things were not always so harmonious. When alone I would spend hours looking through books, I have always taken a keen interest in the Royal Family and I soon acquired a large collection of books about them. Also I would talk to my pretend sister while I did some digging in the garden or scribbling with a pencil. If I managed to get hold of a pair of scissors I would cut up any paper I could find, this included once, much to Bernard's horror, a pack of playing cards.

When I was a child I had a rather nasty temper so that was the reason I had my bottom smacked occasionally, not because I was naughty.

I was unable to walk because of my left leg, also I could not manage the toilet or dress myself. But I could wash my face and feet and even manage a little more when I was in the bath, I could clean my teeth too with my left foot. At this point I would like to make it perfectly clear that I was never at any time trained to use my feet either by my family or anyone else, it all came naturally. Also from a very early age I referred to my feet as hands.

My first experience of a summer holiday was in a caravan

at Heacham which Bernard and I thought was great fun. Another year we went to North Wales to visit Aunt Rene who lived on the coast. I loved playing with my bucket and spade on the beach but would only paddle at the edge of the sea as the larger waves frightened me. It was also during that holiday that I made my first real friend. Aunt Rene took us to meet some friends of hers, the Williamses, who had two children, Myra and Brian. Myra was a pretty dark-haired child, only a few months older than myself. As we were leaving my mother suggested that Myra and I become pen-pals. This we did and soon after Aunt Rene brought Myra to stay with us. Our friendship has lasted through the years and in 1967 my family and I went to Myra's wedding.

Dr Devlin always said, "I want to see her getting around like other children." So just before my fifth birthday I returned to Great Ormond Street Hospital to see what could be made for me.

Nanna (my grandmother) accompanied Mother and me on our trips to London which had to be made by public transport. Besides being expensive this was not an easy journey with luggage and me, also I was terrified of trains. We then had to stay somewhere for one night at least. I always took my black doll, Topsy, for company, but each time my Aunt Edith visited me I would ask when I could go home. She would say the next time she came she would take me but sometimes I had to wait several weeks before her promise came true. How she managed with me alone on the return journey to Norfolk I cannot imagine as I insisted on taking all my toys home, I would not even leave any books behind for the other children.

To return to my stay in Hospital in 1948. Hamley's, the

toy manufacturers, agreed to make something for me and so a car was designed with the doctor's advice. Hamley's not only made the car they gave it to me; the manager brought it along to the Hospital and presented it to me. It was a red car with a steering rod to which my left foot was strapped and a pedal which I operated with my right foot.

I was soon whizzing along the corridors of the Hospital. I remember one day being stopped by a doctor and sent back as I had strayed into a part of the Hospital I should not have been in. I spent many happy hours in that car and used it until I could no longer fit into the seat. Hamley's will never know how much pleasure their gift gave me.

Two other events stand out in my memory of my visits to Great Ormond Street. The first occasion was when they made a film of me doing the things I was able to manage such as feeding myself. The second memory was when Princess Alexandra was also a patient and her mother, the late Princess Marina, visited her. Our beds were wheeled out into the verandah so we could see her, but as our ward was several floors from the ground we only had a glimpse of Princess Marina so we were very disappointed.

When Dr Devlin returned to Ireland his practice was taken over by a younger man, Dr Bree. He was a big man with dark hair and a swarthy complexion. There was certainly no reason for me to dislike him as he was always very nice but I was most unco-operative and cried whenever he visited me. He brought me sweets to try to win me round but he never succeeded.

When I was a child I fell out of my pushchair a few times but I would never agree to being strapped in. After Aunt Queenie moved into a council house Bernard would wheel me round to see her and I fell out of my chair occasionally on these walks. He says I never spoke, but until he picked me up I would look at him as if to say, "Whatever did you do that for?"

During term-time I would pedal my car along the pavement as far as the school to see the children in the playground. Often when I was turning round to go home I would get wedged against the railings and Bernard would have to give me a push. Sometimes Mrs Green, the infant teacher, would ask me inside while she read a story or the children played games such as charades.

By this time the problem of my education was becoming urgent as I was fast approaching my sixth birthday. The ideal thing would have been for me to attend the village school. But my mother was told that the man who was headmaster at that time refused to take me.

The solution to the problem was home tuition and so an official from the Norfolk Education Committee visited us to discuss the arrangements with my parents. It was decided that after school had closed for the day a teacher, Miss Trenowath, would come to give me an hour's tuition four times a week. However this arrangement had to be deferred for a few weeks as my grandfather was suddenly taken ill and died.

Miss Trenowath began teaching me early in May and we quickly settled into a routine. In those early weeks our work was, of course, very elementary but gradually we progressed to more difficult work. However, my tuition ended after only five months.

Mr Haggas, my father's employer, said, "My son has hired a farm and I would like you to be his foreman. Are you agreeable to go?"

As our house had only just been improved my mother was not too happy about moving into a smaller and isolated place. But the move was only to be for five years then Mr Haggas hoped to change to a larger farm. However, by that time his father had died so he returned to Gayton and the farm at Gateley was then hired by a Mr Rivett.

My mother was also concerned about leaving Nanna but my aunt agreed to return home from London to look after her and my other single aunts and uncle. It was also arranged for Bernard to live with them until the following summer because it was felt that a change of schools might unsettle him. This would be a bad thing as he was nearly due to take his 11-plus exam.

And so after considerable thought my parents agreed to the move; therefore in October 1949 we came to Gateley.

3
Childhood Memories

At one time Gateley had been a thriving community of two hundred and fifty people but it gradually grew smaller until it was no more than a hamlet set in the heart of the countryside. The remaining dwellings, twenty-one houses and four farms, were widely scattered about the rolling farmland. The Hall became the country home of a member of the well-known banking family of Hoare. The blacksmith's forge, now no longer standing, was opposite the small church which was reached by walking through part of a farmyard.

The church is now used only for a monthly Holy Communion service and that is only sparsely attended. Even the sheep have gone that once roamed amongst the over-grown graves. But the dominant feature still remains. It is the clock-tower of Sennowe Hall, home of the late Sir Thomas and Lady Cook, which can be seen in the distance rising above the trees.

The only bus that came through the village was one on a Thursday evening for people to go to the cinema in the nearby town of East Dereham and eventually that stopped running. The nearest shops were about three miles away in the neighbouring village of Great Ryburgh, but fortunately the tradespeople ran an efficient delivery service to the out-lying areas. Also from Ryburgh there was a train

service to the market towns of Dereham and Fakenham.
This has since been replaced, as it has in other rural areas,
by a bus service that still by-passes many of the more
isolated villages.

Our new home was one of a pair of red brick cottages
with slate roofs, built in 1862. They were unmodernised
and at first we had to use paraffin lamps as there was no
mains electricity until 1961. However from 1955 we made
our own electricity with a generator which was powered with
a diesel engine. A well stood in a corner of the back garden
and every drop of water we used had to be cranked up from
it in a bucket hooked on to a chain. Each cottage consisted
of a kitchen in which stood the old fashioned cooking-range,
a living-room and three bedrooms.

The houses were set well back from the road as most of
the large garden was at the front. The high-hedged lane
that ran by the side of our neighbour's house led to the
Manor Farm where my father worked.

Bernard has also been employed at Manor Farm ever
since he left school apart from the three years he served as
a dog handler in the R.A.F. police. In recent years he has
taken over from our father as the foreman.

Once a month we made the journey to Gayton to visit
our relatives. This meant walking to Ryburgh from where
we were able to go by train to King's Lynn, from there we
caught the bus to Gayton. The return journey was made by
taxi, bus and finally another taxi. It was a tedious way of
making a journey of only 18 miles so in May 1950 we had
our first family car, a maroon Standard. Later a car became
a real necessity as it was virtually impossible to take my
wheelchair on buses.

A few days after our arrival at Gateley my mother

answered a knock at the door to find a tall, dark-haired young woman standing on the doorstep. It was my new teacher, Ann Ballantyne, who was the infant teacher at Ryburgh school.

Miss Ballantyne (later to become Mrs Colls) taught me for an hour each weekday evening apart from the breaks for the school holidays. During those few hours we covered a surprisingly wide range of subjects, they included Art and Religion as well as the more usual Arithmetic and English. One evening my parents heard me having a reading lesson, I was doing so well that my father felt certain that it was a book I had read many times before. So after Miss Ballantyne had left he tested me by telling me to read an item from the newspaper. Imagine the expression on his face when I read it word perfect.

At various intervals the Senior Educational Psychologist would visit me to see how my school-work was progressing. Mr Thomson was a tall, broad-shouldered man who spoke softly with a slight burr of his native Scotland. In addition to written papers he gave me oral speed-tests, both of which I answered with reasonable success.

During one of Mr Thomson's visits he offered to find me a pen-friend. In fact he sent me the addresses of two girls, both able-bodied, who lived in Wood Green. One of them soon stopped writing but the other girl, Pamela Turner, corresponded with me for several years before we drifted apart. However, I was to hear from Pam again some ten years later.

On another occasion Mr Thomson asked me to send an essay to Dr Lincoln Ralphs, the Chief Education Officer for Norfolk. Mrs Colls suggested the subject, the marriage of the then Princess Elizabeth to the Duke of Edinburgh. I illustrated my story with paintings of the main participants in the event, the paintings were poor but the colours and styles of the clothes were authentic. Dr Ralphs wrote to me saying how pleased he was to have an example of my work.

I have never met Dr Ralphs but he has always given me every possible help he could through the years. I am indebted to him for this and for his assistance in compiling information for this book.

In 1950, with Mrs Colls' help but unbeknown to my parents, I wrote to Princess Elizabeth after the announcement that she was expecting her second baby. As the Princess was staying in Malta her lady-in-waiting replied on notepaper headed Villa Guardemangia. But I was most thrilled with the enclosed picture of Prince Charles on his mother's knee.

The same year I received my second letter from a member of the Royal Family. This time I had written to Princess Margaret on learning that on July 22nd she was to attend a St John Ambulance Brigade rally at Sennowe Park.

A short distance inside the main gate of the park one crosses a bridge over the river Wensum which runs through the grounds. Then comes a steep hill before the ground levels out into the extensive wooded parkland which surrounds the house and lake. It was on this hill that our car stalled and my mother could not get it to start again. Fortunately a coach driver came to our rescue and eventually we crawled up the hill.

In the bright sunlight the park made a perfect setting for the memorable occasion. The petite Princess looked most attractive in her uniform as Commandant-in-Chief; by her side as she inspected the cadets was the stocky figure of Sir Thomas in his uniform as County Commissioner of the Brigade.

As we strolled around the gardens after the inspection we met Lord and Lady Romney. It was then we learned that at Lady Romney's request it had been arranged for me to meet the Princess, but at the appointed time we could not be found. And so I missed the chance of a lifetime.

To help make up a little for my disappointment my family had a large colour photograph of Princess Margaret framed for me. In it the Princess is wearing the rose-sprayed gown she wore for her twentieth-birthday photographs. This still hangs in my bedroom as also on my dressing-table stands the photograph of Queen Elizabeth II which Bernard gave me at the time of her Coronation.

Apart from having home tuition my childhood continued much the same as any other child's. I played with John, the boy next door, who had dark curly hair and an attractive dimpled smile. Our favourite game was Cowboys and Indians and for that my car became a bucking bronco.

In the evenings Bernard and I often played football. We used a large wool ball which had to be kicked between the legs of a chair for a goal. I would sit directly in front of my goal but Bernard could squeeze the ball past me to score. However that was before I started to put on weight.

Bernard and his friend Brian Noy, who had inherited his pale complexion and auburn hair from his mother, spent hours playing together with their Meccano sets. I would help them by finding the various green-painted pieces, wheels and axles they used in the construction of numerous machines and gadgets.

My parents had made friends with Molly and Walter Pearce whose farm was only a short distance from our house. Molly, who was in her mid-thirties with black, tightly curling hair, always had a smile on her plump, bespectacled face. Walter was a quiet big-boned man who was going bald. They became friends in the true sense of the word as also did the Noys who were slightly older than my parents. Stockily built Arthur Noy with his greying hair brushed straight back was always to be found wreathed in clouds of smoke from his beloved pipe.

Molly joined Maud Noy, mother and me on the boys' school outings. These included a tour of London in 1953 to see the Coronation decorations prior to a journey by launch down the river to Kew Gardens.

When my cousins, especially Betty, came to stay they would take me for walks, weather permitting, in the upright wheelchair I then had. We went miles along the quiet roads which were laced with the patterns made by the sun filtering through the leaves of the trees.

Betty also stayed with us one Christmas. We still laugh about how we kept awake for as long as we could, talking and keeping "Father Christmas" waiting.

Betty was staying too when my father's employer, Murray Rivett, asked us to live in the farmhouse while he and his wife were abroad on holiday. All went smoothly until Betty had returned home and then I had a frightening experience. I used to scoff at ghost stories but not any more.

The first night I slept alone I heard footsteps going down the passage from Bernard's bedroom, which was next to mine, to the bathroom. I thought it was Bernard but then they continued along the passage until they stopped outside my door. The room was light enough for me to see the door-knob begin to turn very, very slowly. I lay and watched in terror for what seemed like minutes but it could have only been a few seconds. Then as the door started to open I screamed.

I made so much noise that I could not hear Bernard calling to me. The strange thing was that my mother found my door still tightly shut as she had left it. She had to sleep with me not only for the rest of that night but for the remainder of our stay at the farm. Although this happened all those years ago I am still firmly convinced that I heard and saw exactly what I have just described. Moreover I now know that the house has long had the reputation of being haunted.

But to return to more usual events. My uncle Charles, a big man with a ruddy complexion and thinning hair, sometimes joined me for tea-parties. At these I poured tea from my doll's tea-set and we ate jam-tarts which I had made from scraps of my mother's pastry. I realise how honoured I should have felt when my uncle actually ate the tarts as nobody is more particular about his food than he is.

In Coronation year Betty's youngest sister, Diane, was born. I found that I was able to hold her by cradling her to me with her head resting in the crook of my right knee. This is quite safe when a baby is small but I cannot manage to hold them after they get more active. Once by propping Diane up on the settee with cushions I managed to feed her with her bottle.

I usually found a way of doing things. For instance I used scissors when top-and-tailing gooseberries. And when I was given my first watch it seemed perfectly natural to me to wear it strapped around my ankle.

My mother taught me to knit and this I enjoyed doing. In recent years I have won prizes for my knitting at exhibitions of handicrafts made by disabled people. I prefer to make small garments and although I am a slower knitter than the average person I can manage lacy patterns.

But I was not so successful at first as this amusing incident shows. I had been knitting for nearly a whole afternoon before I realised that my work had not grown. We soon discovered that I had been slipping the stitches instead of knitting them. I never made that mistake again.

My writing had been big and scrawly but with extra care it became smaller and neater, however it was some years before I added the more adult loops and whirls. I use a ball-point pen as I have never managed to use a fountain-pen so well.

Garth Colls sometimes collected his wife after our lessons ended. He played the clarinet in a local dance band and if he was too early he would practise while he waited in the lane. Perhaps it was this that prompted Mrs Colls to suggest that I learn music. The Education Committee supplied me with a dulcimer which they considered was the most suitable instrument for me to play. And so music lessons were added to an already tight schedule.

The dulcimer was placed on the floor, then I was able to play it with the wooden hammers held in both feet. I quickly mastered simple tunes such as nursery rhymes and my family encouraged me by giving me the sheet music of some popular tunes. But I was too impatient to finish with the elementary exercises and go on to more interesting pieces. Thereafter my interest waned and when my education entered another phase I used it as an excuse to give up music.

Looking back I regret this but wanting to rush things has always been a failing of mine. However I can be just as obstinate and see a thing through particularly if the odds are against me.

4
School Days

Mrs Colls taught me for three and a half years until the spring of 1953. Then an official from the Education Committee came to tell us that it was felt at long last that there was no reason why I should not attend an ordinary school. Of course we were delighted about this decision as it was what we had always hoped for.

It was suggested that I should go to the school in the nearby village of Guist as it was the one Bernard attended. But because a car took the Gateley children to Ryburgh school my mother thought the latter would be more suitable. And so she went to see the headmaster, Mervyn White.

Mr White was in his forties, of average build with thinning hair, he was an extremely tolerant person and an excellent teacher. He agreed to my attending his school and arranged to collect my mother and me in his car one evening so that I could see the school. Mrs Colls also accompanied us on our tour.

The sprawling red-brick building divided the playground into two areas, the smaller one at the back being for the infants only. The plaque outside on the wall beneath the clock-tower was erected to commemorate the Coronation of Edward VIIth and the ending of the Boer War. A low brick wall surrounded the playground, on top of it was close-mesh wire which was intended to stop balls being kicked into the road, however it was not completely successful.

Both the boys' and girls' cloakrooms led into the senior classroom, this was a large airy room with high windows which offered no distractions to the pupils. The remaining two classrooms which were smaller led off from that room and the rectangular assembly hall was at the far end. This was used too for dancing and for games during the winter. Also, as the kitchen adjoined it, the hall was converted into a dining-room by setting out trestle tables and bench seats.

Mr White taught the older children so I was to be in his class. A middle-aged woman with neat grey hair, Mrs Barnes, was in charge of the juniors, and as I have previously stated Ann Colls was the infant teacher.

It was arranged that I would travel to and from school each day with the other children. My wheelchair could be left at the school in term-time for Mr White to lift me from the car to this in the morning and vice versa in the afternoon. It was agreed that I could sit at the lunch-table that Mrs Colls supervised and she was also to take me to the toilet. Later when she was expecting her baby – it turned out to be twins – Mrs Barnes took over the latter. The only special equipment I needed was a low desk which was moved out of the infants' classroom for me.

My mother took me to school on my first morning, April 11th. Mr White met us in the playground I remember and took me into school telling my mother that there was no need for her to wait around. He obviously wondered if I would be upset by this complete change in my life. But he need not have worried, I am sure that first day seemed longer to my mother than it did to me.

It's true that school life did seem a little strange but there were so many interesting things happening. I soon settled into the routine and made many friends who were quite happy to wheel me about whenever it was necessary.

One girl, Jennifer Howe, a plump, dark-haired, cheerful person, a little older than myself, was also in a wheelchair so we had a lot in common. We used to spend an occasional day visiting each other during the school holidays.

Another close friend was Jean Adams, a pretty girl who wore her thick dark hair cut short. Poor Jean was very upset one day when I fell out of my chair as she was wheeling me out of the dining-room. How it happened I have no idea but it was definitely not through any fault of Jean's. I was not hurt at all but Mr White insisted that I spend the afternoon resting in his house which was situated next to the school. Jean also had an afternoon free from lessons as Mr White agreed to my request that she be allowed to keep me company.

Obviously there were certain activities I could not take part in, one of these was dancing. Mrs Barnes took my classmates for this while Mr White gave her pupils reading lessons. At first I passed these periods by reading too but after a while I was allowed to assist Mr White by hearing some of the better readers.

But I was able to compete in the game of rounders by hitting the ball with a table-tennis bat and having someone run for me. My right leg has always been strong so I was able to hit the ball hard, at the same time trying to keep it low as I aimed at any gap between the fielders. And I shouted instructions to my runner as to whether they should wait or not before running to the next circle. I was quite

The Author

successful at the game but naturally I used to choose the volunteer who could run the fastest.

Mrs Barnes instructed the girls in needlework. Through those lessons I developed a liking for embroidery which lasted several years. I used to do a lot at one time but then I became tired of it and returned to knitting. I still have one article I made at school, it's a handkerchief satchet which I embroidered with flowers and my name.

Some of my friends and I amused ourselves at playtime by acting small plays we made up; we never had a proper script, just an outline of a plot. I must have a bossy streak in me as I was always in charge of our productions as well as having a leading rôle in them. The headmaster gave us every encouragement; he gave permission for us to rehearse in the assembly hall and even allowed us to perform our plays in front of the assembled pupils at the end of each term. I thoroughly enjoyed organising our little efforts.

Once a year the school gave an official concert for the parents; it was held in the modern Village Hall. I had a part in one of the plays performed by the senior class, usually as one of a group of courtiers or something similar. So I was thrilled when I was eventually given a larger speaking part which was suitable for me as it involved no moving around. I concentrated on learning my lines until I was word perfect.

Then only a few days before the concert I developed an abscess in my left ear. Although I was in considerable pain I wanted to carry on but Dr Arthur, our elderly family doctor, was firmly against the idea. It was about ten years before I appeared on stage again and then it was in something completely different.

Dr Arthur was very kind to me on the few occasions I

needed him professionally. If I had influenza he would absent-mindedly ask me if I had any pains in my *arms* and legs, this greatly amused me; but I am sure that he never realised that he had said anything odd.

Only one interesting event happened outside my school life during that time. The Ministry decided to provide me with some kind of self-propelling vehicle as well as my wheelchair. A technician came to take measurements and assess my capabilities and after several weeks the machine arrived.

It was a low, open, three-wheeler tricycle which I operated by pedalling with my right foot. My left foot was strapped to a rod which I moved to change gear, the steering I did with my back. It was rather heavy and cumbersome for me to manage as there was very little flat road for me to go on, so it was not a great success.

However I do recall one incident that occurred shortly after I had the tricycle. Bernard was out for a walk with me, we were coming down a hill near our house when I suddenly realised that he had dropped back and was quite a distance behind me. By that time I was gathering speed and quickly losing control. So I steered towards the grass bank and hoped for the best; fortunately I did not turn over. It seems funny now but it was not at the time.

About eighteen months after commencing at Ryburgh school I was amongst the group of pupils who completed a general knowledge test paper. As I did not realise it was the preliminary paper for the 11-plus examination my parents only knew about it the day before the actual exam took place. At my first attempt I was a border line failure which gave me the opportunity for another try the following February. That time I passed both papers. On each occasion I sat for the exam under identical conditions to the other children.

My success created yet another problem. Dr Ralphs wrote to my parents explaining that it was not possible for me to attend Fakenham Grammar School but he promised to look into alternative methods of instruction.

The letter was soon followed by an official from the Education Committee accompanied by Mr White. The official told my mother that the nearest school for physically handicapped children to include grammar school standard in its curriculum was in Yorkshire. Naturally neither my family nor I were too happy about it as it was so far from home. But Mr White pointed out what a great pity it would be for me not to continue my education. The official stated bluntly that the authorities could do nothing more for me if I refused to go to Yorkshire, so we eventually agreed to at least visit the school.

And so on a beautiful summer's day I saw for the first time the school that was to be my second home for nearly two years.

5
Welburn Hall

Welburn Hall Special School is situated in the North Riding of Yorkshire. It stands in large wooded grounds only a short distance from the village of Kirbymoorside which is approximately thirty miles north of York.

My father's employer, Murray Rivett, a well-built man in his late thirties with curly hair, drove my parents and myself on our first visit to the school.

It was still early morning when we set off on the long journey. Our route was through the flat, open countryside of Lincolnshire with its twisting roads before we reached the hills of Yorkshire. It was a county that I soon grew to love with its friendly people and picturesque landscape that is scarred in places with coal-mines and slag-heaps.

It was mid-morning when we entered the main gateway which was of wrought iron supported by stone pillars. We drove past the lodge which housed one of the teachers and his family as also did the lodge at the back entrance to the school. We passed along an avenue of tall trees underneath which large golden daffodils bloomed in the spring. The driveway crossed a bridge over the river, which ran through the grounds, before sweeping between smooth green lawns to the courtyard in front of the long grey stone hall.

I waited alone in the car while my parents talked with the

headmaster in his study. I doubt if the interview lasted half an hour but to me it seemed much longer. I was glad of the diversion when a few of the older pupils, some walking, others in wheelchairs, came over to the main building during their mid-morning break.

At about the same time a small but strong looking man in his late forties approached the car to offer me an orange drink. The man had a tanned complexion and straight hair, he wore a white tunic style overall. He told me he was one of the nursing orderlies, as his surname was Skipper he was called "Skip" by both the children and staff.

I had finished my drink by the time my parents returned to the car. They were accompanied by the headmaster, Hywel Williams, who was obviously a Welshman. He was a kindly looking middle-aged man of average build with a thick mane of grey hair. He usually wore green tweeds and I do not recollect ever seeing him outside without his cap.

We began our tour of the school by strolling round the grounds which looked beautiful bathed in the summer sunshine. A door in the high wall led around to the other side of the Hall where there were more velvet-like lawns. Stone steps ran down from the terrace to a gravelled walk between yew bushes to the lake. This was converted into a swimming-pool some years later.

The pathway ran parallel with the Hall. In one direction it led towards the headmaster's house which was a short distance from the school buildings. In the opposite direction the path joined a rough roadway which followed the course of the river with its small but attractive waterfall. By walking along there we eventually reached the main driveway once again and so completed the square back to the courtyard in front of the Hall.

Before inspecting the classrooms we went inside the Hall. As shallow steps led up to the main door we used a side entrance where a wooden ramp had been fitted for the pupils in wheelchairs.

The downstairs rooms were large and airy with stone-flagged floors. The main room had originally been an entrance hall but was now used for evening assembly, Sunday morning service and film shows on Saturday afternoons. It was a big room with window seats under the long windows which were all along one side of the room. At the far end was a huge open stone fireplace which was used during the winter.

Leading off from there were dormitories for the younger children, Sister's office and a small surgery. (Down the corridor was the senior common room.) Beside the fireplace a ramp ran down to the dining-room, each table seated six people. Also on that lower level were the kitchens, staff dining-room and TV room. Here too was a telephone booth for the pupils to use.

We met Sister, a kindly, middle-aged woman with grey hair whose name was Welburn, which was most appropriate. She told us that the rest of the medical staff consisted of four nurses who were on duty two at a time, two male orderlies whose duties included all heavy lifting and carrying pupils up and down stairs, also there was a night sister. A local doctor attended any sick children whenever it was necessary and a dentist visited the school regularly.

After our talk with Sister we went upstairs to see the dormitory I would occupy if I decided to attend the school. It was a long, cheerful-looking room with flowered curtains at the three large windows. The walls and paintwork were cream as also were the iron bedsteads, these were covered

with a green bedspread similar to those used in hospitals.
At the side of each bed stood a locker for personal belongings.

Other rooms on the first floor consisted of the remaining
dormitories, the headmaster's study, a well-stocked tuck-
shop, library, infants' classroom, staff rooms and finally a
darkroom which could be used by the seniors who were
interested in photography.

There were more staff rooms on the top floor. It was here
where our clothes were stored on their return from the
laundry, a clean set was handed out to us at the end of
the week. I learned much later that in the summer a certain
amount of storing favourite dresses, etc., in lockers for
special occasions went on. This meant that another dress, or
whatever the garment was, would have to be worn for a
fortnight. Of course it needed washing before then so the
girl concerned had to do it herself. Which explains why
several articles of clothing could be seen at most weekends,
hanging out of bathroom windows, drying or airing in the
warm sunshine.

Mr Williams then took us across to the classrooms. They
were wooden constructions built around the sides of a
cobbled square that had once been a stable-yard. Here too
was a small, cosy room that was used mainly by the pupils
who were studying for G.C.E. A-level exams. These buildings were reached by way of a steep concrete ramp which
saved a long walk round the driveway. The yard also gave
access to the kitchen garden and the stables that had not
been demolished; these now housed the pet rabbits owned
by some of the children.

Two of the four classrooms were occupied by the junior
scholars, the remaining ones were where the Secondary and

Grammar syllabus were taught. However there was a certain amount of inter-changing of rooms and teachers for various lessons.

We visited each of the classes in turn and were introduced to the teachers. Although at the time names and faces were little more than a blur I will pause here to give a brief description of those I became most closely associated with.

Firstly there was Mr Booker who, in addition to teaching S1, which would be my class, specialised in teaching geography, music and French. He was a likeable man, tall with dark hair, he was in his thirties but looked older because of his receding hairline. We always knew when he was annoyed because the tip of his nose would turn white.

Kenneth Boothroyd was the maths, biology and chemistry teacher. He was a humorous, middle-aged person with a pleasant creased face; he was of stocky build with wavy hair.

Miss Caygill's subject was Latin. She was probably in her mid-forties, a fair-haired woman with a beautiful soft skin. I presume her favourite colour was green as she was often dressed in it.

Miss Taylor was young with shoulder-length dark hair. She taught history, needlework and art. Mr Williams took the English classes himself.

Now we return to my story. When we had finished our tour of the school we thanked the headmaster for all the help and information he had given us. As it was lunch-time he suggested that I join the other children but we explained that we ought to be starting our long journey, we would stop for a meal on the way.

I liked Welburn with its beautiful grounds and happy

atmosphere that had been immediately apparent. I felt that I could be happy there too.

And so on November 3rd, 1955, after the half-term holiday, I began my two years at boarding school.

6
Life at Boarding School

It was late when my mother and I arrived at Welburn on that dark November evening. But the lights from the windows of the Hall blazed out a warm welcome as our car stopped by the main door.

The Norfolk Education authorities provided the transport for my journeys to and from Yorkshire and we were driven by a Schools Welfare Officer. This was usually Wilfred Hawke, a tall, slim man with straight greying hair and a tanned skin that was stretched tightly across his bony face.

We were all glad of the meal that awaited us that night in the staff dining-room. Afterwards my mother settled me in my dormitory before returning to spend the night at the home of my father's stepbrother, Herbert. He and his wife Betty lived in the small village of Moss which is situated near Doncaster.

Next morning we were awakened at seven o'clock, an hour before breakfast. Lessons started at nine with assembly being held in each classroom.

When I was wheeled into class on my first morning I saw written on the blackboard a few words welcoming me to S1. I really did appreciate that kind gesture of some unknown person.

The routine was simple. We had a mid-morning break and at midday we stopped work for lunch, the food was plentiful and tasty. Classes recommenced at two o'clock and ended at four when we all raced back to the Hall for assembly. This was followed by high tea, then our evenings were free apart from having to do any "prep".

A sandwich supper was optional, but in the winter we preferred to smuggle canned soup or baked beans down to the kitchen to be heated through. These extras were then consumed in the dorms.

Lights-out was at nine o'clock, though two evenings a week we were allowed to stay up late to watch TV. The occupants of each dorm were allowed to choose which nights they liked most.

I never had time to be homesick as I joined the other scholars at an exciting time of year. November 4th is known as Mischief Night in Yorkshire. The name is self-explanatory. Tricks were played on staff and pupils alike and even though I was such a new pupil I got my share of treatment but it was great fun. The most unusual things found their way into beds, and belongings were swapped for someone else's.

The following day the gardeners built a large bonfire surmounted by a guy. In the evening the whole school gathered around it; the teachers supervised the lighting of the fireworks while we watched and ate the traditional parkin.

After all this gaiety life settled back into the normal routine. This gave me the opportunity to make friends. Because I had met few people outside of my immediate family circle I lacked confidence in myself. However I soon made friends, at first it was with those of a quiet nature but I learned after a while to stand on my own two feet and mix with everybody.

It was while I was at Welburn that I was cured of my

temper. I was storming away one day (I cannot recollect why) when I suddenly noticed the shocked faces of my friends. I resolved there and then never to fly into a rage again and I have kept my word. Fortunately I retained enough spirit to hold my own in a discussion and I can fight my own battles!

The members of my class were studying for their "O" levels and so for a while I worked alone. I joined the others for biology which I was always interested in. I did Latin which I loathed with one other girl, Pauline Rogers, a frail looking girl with a sweet smile.

I think it is worth mentioning here that Mervyn White had told me that I had a talent for essay writing, but Mr Williams held the opposite view. I missed the freedom we had in choice of subject at Ryburgh. I found it extremely difficult to write on a given topic, therefore my standard deteriorated.

According to the children Welburn had a ghost, the Grey Lady. I would huddle under the bed-clothes while they described her "walks". Eventually I realised she was only a figment of the imagination and then I too frightened newcomers with tales of her exploits.

Although they had no relatives at the school two of our regular visitors were a middle-aged couple from Middlesbrough. The Cookes were wonderful people who had a great love of children. The small figure of Mr Cooke, his bald head shining in the sun, was often seen playing on the lawns with the children and his beautiful red Irish setter, while his plump, dark-haired wife smilingly looked on.

Visitors were allowed on alternative Saturdays but because of the distance my family could only make the journey once a month. They came for Bank Holidays and half-term when we had a long weekend free. On these occasions I was allowed to stay with them in lodgings nearby. We usually stayed at the home of Miss Jackson, one of the school's cooks. She was a kindly person who allowed us to use her home as if it were our own.

In addition to these visits my mother would telephone me each Friday evening at a set time, I was able to take her call in Sister's office. If the telephone was placed on a chair I could manage unaided. In this way my family and I kept in close touch, which was a good thing as I was very remiss at writing letters home.

As Christmas grew near the feeling of excitement mounted. On the last day of term desks were cleared and cases were packed before we came to the serious business of the day. This was a party followed by a visit from Father Christmas. He was dressed in traditional costume and from his sack he distributed gifts to us all.

Winter halted all outdoor activities so we had to find other forms of amusement in the New Year.

In this we were helped by Kenneth Boothroyd. He sang quite pleasantly to his own guitar accompaniment and so he passed many pleasant evenings for us with his entertainment. He was also making a cine-film of school activities. As well as shooting scenes in the snow, winter gave him the time for cutting and splicing the film, this was an interesting, though slow, process to watch.

Another of Mr Boothroyd's hobbies was writing science fiction stories; he was successful in getting a number of these published in book form. Sometimes, when he came to check that everything was all right before lights-out on the evenings he was duty teacher, we would persuade him to tell us one of his stories. He would light a cigarette and then switch off the lights before beginning. He walked around as he talked, it was eerie listening to his soft voice and watching the red glow of his cigarette. But the moment he sensed someone was genuinely growing nervous he ended abruptly, in spite of our protests, by switching on the lights and talking of something totally different.

Some of the pupils were preparing to be Confirmed. I was asked to join the Confirmation classes but I refused simply because I did not feel ready to take this important step. I have never been a regular churchgoer but religion is important to me and I knew it was wrong to take part feeling as I did.

During the summer months we often walked to church in a neighbouring village for morning service on a Sunday. It was at this beautiful little church surrounded by woods that the simple, yet moving, service took place.

One thing I did join though was the school choir. This has always been a huge family joke as I cannot sing a note. Mr Booker would not let me give it up although he usually noticed someone was off key when I sang; if I stayed quiet all was well. One evening I had to stay behind after practice to go through the scales. It was half an hour later when Mr Booker was finally satisfied. He commented smilingly that if I had not been tone deaf I would have been a good singer as I had an expressive face. I never improved but it taught me to appreciate some of the lighter classics.

The daffodils heralded spring and with it came the chance for outings. These included going to Pickering Grammar School to the plays performed by the pupils there, occasionally we acted as hosts to them at Welburn. Another outing was an afternoon visit to York to see a matinee performance of the ballet "Coppelia".

Then came that beautiful summer of the Suez Crisis. The tension was felt in our sheltered world as we anxiously discussed the situation. As the clouds died away we relaxed and life took on a light-hearted air once more.

One Saturday afternoon a garden fête was being held in the grounds of a nearby house. As it was a bright sunny day a group of us decided to go.

Shortly before we started out the back of my neck began to irritate. I had a strong suspicion what the cause was as several pupils had chicken-pox. But I still went to the fête.

On our return I reported sick. Obviously Sister guessed that I had known about the spots before I went out. After about a fortnight in bed I was allowed up, but I had to spend a few days in the common room before I returned to classes. I was not alone as one of the boys had also reached the convalescent stage.

To while away the long days he offered to teach me to play chess. But as I have never played since I have forgotten all I learned about the game.

Weekends were spent in lazing around or going for long walks. A friend, Audrey Hardy, a large dark-haired girl with a good-natured face, wheeled me in my chair for what seemed like miles along the deserted country roads.

Occasionally I would borrow a swimsuit and cool off in the little fountains, the fountains were turned off and we used the concrete bowls as paddling pools. This was several years before the lake was converted into a swimming pool.

Mrs Booker organised the school's group of Girl Guides of which I was a member. I became quite competent at tying knots and first-aid but when I was tested for my cooking badge it was another matter.

Audrey and I were taking this badge together. So after

giving us the equipment we needed Mrs Booker left us alone in the meadow we used when building fires. Audrey started by cutting a large square of turf which she carefully removed. We then built the sticks in a pyramid inside the hole before attempting to light them with the permitted two matches. Although I lay on the grass and tried to fan the fire into flames with my breath it was hopeless.

Fortunately we managed to attract the attention of two boys and they got us some more matches from a member of the staff. When the fire was burning brightly we melted some fat in the frying-pan. We had sausages and bread to fry so we cooked the sausages first. Or tried to! The skins rapidly turned black but we found that they were still raw inside. Also the fire had nearly burnt out.

At that critical moment we saw Mrs Booker coming back to check us. We knew we would fail and neither of us felt like going through all that again. There was only one thing to be done. With a well-aimed shot I threw the sausages into some nearby bushes.

Mrs Booker doubtfully eyed the soggy piece of bread. However, she passed us as she thought we had eaten the sausages so she presumed they must have been palatable.

But our cheating did not really matter as my Section had to prepare tea when we had a day camping. And even I could shell hard boiled eggs without spoiling them.

After I had been at Welburn about a year the arrangements were changed for my journey home to Norfolk for holidays. Sister visited a relative at Cambridge, so she suggested that I travel with her by train to Peterborough where Mr Hawke could meet me. This was much better particularly during the winter.

Being away from home had taught me to be more independent. At home I had been sliding downstairs on my bottom for some time but I now found that I was not able to get upstairs unaided. This was because the school stairs were shallow and divided into short flights by landings. By going backwards and pushing down with my right foot I could lift myself from step to step.

I could heave myself on to the toilet too by swinging up with my left shoulder in the way I used to climb on to a chair. By this method I could get on to the side of the bath, then I could slide into it. Audrey could get me out again by first standing me on one leg, then swinging me on to the floor.

Rules were broken the same as they are at any other boarding school. I must not give away too many secrets but here are a few of our misdemeanours.

Our walks were often along roads that were out of bounds. At weekends we would try to stay awake to listen to a late night programme of Top Twenty records on my radio: we usually fell asleep. And, of course, we held the traditional midnight feasts in our dorms.

However, one autumn evening something more serious happened but whether it was an accident or a prank we never knew. It did prove though that if there was a fire we could escape to safety in a few minutes.

Periodically we would have a fire drill practice. When the alarm sounded we had to assemble in the common room as quickly as possible. This exercise was always conducted with speed and efficiency, but as the staff were pre-warned it did not indicate what would really happen in an emergency.

When the alarm rang that particular evening there seemed to be nothing unusual about it. But when we reached the common room we realised this time was different as the staff had aroused the younger children who were already in bed.

Mr Williams made the roll-call; six girls were missing. A quick but unsuccessful search was made for them. We discovered some time later that they were visiting Mrs Williams when the alarm sounded. On hearing it she insisted that they remain at the cottage which was understandable but it only added to her husband's anxiety.

By the time the firemen arrived a search had revealed that there was no fire in the building. Someone had sounded the alarm either accidentally or deliberately. It was the only time I saw Mr Williams annoyed: he was furious. But the officers were understanding and made no charge for their unnecessary journey.

The culprit was never found. Even the school grapevine failed to give a clue to his identity. Perhaps it was lucky for him or her that they were not found out as it would have meant serious trouble for them.

I had been joined in class by two boys so we moved into the library for our lessons. I was held back for a time until they caught up to my standard. I believe that is what will happen if the comprehensive system of education is adopted, therefore, I am strongly opposed to it.

Luckily, however, this boring period only lasted a short while as my time at Welburn was nearing its end.

7
Chapel Allerton

It all began one bright summer afternoon in 1957, when the school physiotherapist unexpectedly collected me from my classroom.

On our way over to the Hall, she explained that a specialist from a Leeds hospital had come to see one of the infant children, Patrick. My name had been mentioned during the conversation, with the result that the specialist, a Mr Thomson, had asked to see me.

Mr Thomson was waiting for us in the headmaster's study. He was a large man who had a habit of peering over the top of his spectacles, without speaking a word. This, together with his gruff voice, was most disconcerting, although he was really a very nice person.

After a brief examination he told me that, provided I was prepared to work hard, he was sure that I could be fitted with some kind of apparatus which would enable me to walk. I would have to visit the out-patients department at his hospital, then after my equipment was made I would be admitted to the hospital for training. But my stay would probably be for little more than a fortnight; in that he was grossly over-optimistic.

I received this news with no comment which seemed to baffle Mr Thomson and Mr Williams. But the news had been so unexpected that it took several minutes for me to realise fully what it all meant. Also, the deeper I felt about something the less emotion I showed.

Later, when I tried to analyse my feelings I found it difficult. Before now I had hardly thought about my disability, it had never bothered me in any way, it was something that I had accepted as there had seemed to be nothing that could be done about it. True, I had sometimes felt it was a damn' nuisance if it had stopped me doing something that I had wanted to do, but that was all. Certainly I had seen no point in making my life a misery over it and consequently the lives of those close to me.

But now this was all changed. Of course, the prospect of being able to walk was wonderful but nevertheless I felt some slight apprehension. My main concern was, how could I walk and at the same time use my feet as hands?

That evening I tried to write to my parents telling them of my news. Somehow I just could not find the right words. I knew how much it would mean to them and I was afraid of raising their hopes too high. In the end I decided to wait until our weekly chat on the telephone, but by the Friday evening they had received a letter from Mr Thomson.

The date was arranged for my day's visit to Leeds. The hospital was Chapel Allerton, which incorporated a Ministry of Pensions limb-fitting centre. My visit that day was to the Centre. I travelled by ambulance, together with the school's physiotherapist and little Patrick. He had been born with short, deformed legs, one of his arms was perfectly normal but the other ended at the elbow. He had visited the Centre on several previous occasions and was to get his artificial legs that day.

The morning was mainly devoted to Patrick who looked

very proud as he tried his new legs. Apart from a short interview with Mr Thomson I was left sitting around, watching the hustle and bustle of that busy Centre. The place had a peculiar smell of its own, I suppose it was the new leather and tin of all the assorted equipment and gadgets. After a lunch of sandwiches it was my turn for attention.

I was attended to by Frank, a short, slim man whose hair was sparse although he was probably still in his thirties.

Frank sent me up to the hospital, which stood on higher ground, for me to be extensively X-rayed. On my return Frank himself took a number of measurements, before he made a plaster cast of my left leg.

It was late when we returned to Welburn, most of the pupils were in bed. I was tired and hungry, the swaying motion of the ambulance had increased my feeling of nausea. But, after a light meal, I felt more refreshed and was in better spirits by the time my mother telephoned.

She had already rung the school twice that evening, so was anxious to know why I had been so late in getting back. In the privacy of the headmaster's study I was able to give her a brief summary of the day's events.

I still had mixed feelings about the whole venture. Finding it difficult to discuss them with either family or friends, I decided to confide in someone I was never likely to meet. So I wrote to Douglas Bader, the legless wartime fighter pilot, who had become a legend in his life-time, and was now such an example to other disabled people.

Although I had been vague as to where to address my letter to him, I received a reply without much delay. His letter was a lengthy one, full of advice and encouragement, which I found a great help.

It was eventually arranged, to everyone's satisfaction, that I should go into hospital for my training in September, instead of returning to Welburn in the usual way. As I was only expected to be there for a short time it would cause very little disruption to my education.

The authorities agreed for Mr Hawke to drive my mother and myself as usual. Even though events did not go according to plan, they were good in this respect, and continued to provide transport for most of my journeys to and from Leeds in the next two years.

I had been extremely happy during my two years at Welburn and when I said goodbye to all my friends as we started our summer holiday break, I looked forward to my return there.

I felt strangely apprehensive as we began our journey to Leeds that September morning in 1957. I kept this feeling to myself, it seemed so silly as I was used to being away from home. I was quiet during the journey and I grew even more so – if that was possible – as we neared our destination.

On my previous visit to Leeds I had not seen much of the city from inside the ambulance. Now as we drove through its outskirts I looked around me with interest.

It was like so many other industrial towns, with its streets of small, dark houses, huddled together as if trying to hide from the sooty smoke which belched forth from the factory chimneys. Across the short side streets hung lines of washing while children played in the gutters. Here and there could be seen the towering blocks of new flats in which some of these families would be rehoused. These were sometimes built with so much lack of thought and planning, that it was only replacing one slum with another.

Chapel Allerton was situated on the other side of the

city. Here the houses were brighter, with their neat front gardens and dainty net curtains at the windows. There were even stunted trees standing along the sides of the roads like sentries.

The hospital consisted of a large grey-stone building on the left of the tarmac drive and, scattered around it further along, a number of wooden huts. Green lawns were pleasantly shaded by tall trees, underneath them squirrels happily played. The borders were gaily filled with red and blue flowers.

A sign directed us to the enquiry office in the main building. This was joined to a cluster of huts by a steeply sloping passage-way, which was covered in as protection against the elements. From the office we were sent to one of these huts, Ward H.

The passage-way joined at right-angles with a shorter corridor which led straight into the ward. The bathrooms, small ward kitchen and sister's office were along the corridor. The ward itself looked like any other with its regimented rows of beds along each side. Down the middle of the ward were radiators interspaced with dining-tables, around which some of the patients were sitting, having their evening meal.

Sister Lawson, who was in charge of Ward H, was off-duty when we arrived. In her absence we were greeted by the Staff Nurse, Olive Dobson.

"Dobby" was an attractive person of small build, with fine features and beautiful dark eyes. She was probably in her early forties but already her dark hair was threaded with silver.

There was only time for a quick farewell before my mother had to leave. It was better that way as by then I had succumbed to my feelings and was in tears, which must have been unsettling for my mother's peace of mind. When she left, "Dobby" was trying to comfort me, though her own eyes were suspiciously moist. I came to realise that this was so typical of her, she had a deep compassion for her fellow-beings. It is a rare quality but one that is found in all the best nurses and doctors.

When I had recovered my composure "Dobby" introduced me to the people who were sitting at one of the tables. Then she left me to eat my meal as I assured her I was able to feed myself. I soon found, however, that the table was too high for me to manage properly. But my problem was short-lived as one of the other patients offered to help me.

I learned that the woman's name was Edna Coote. She was a plump, middle-aged woman with fair hair that hung loosely to her shoulders. She became my self-appointed helper and always kept a motherly eye on me.

During the coming weeks and months, "Dobby" and Edna became dear to me. Whenever I had any problems or worries I would turn to them. Looking back I realise that they gave me much good advice, though I doubt if I always thought so at the time.

After we had finished our meal some of the patients told me a little about the hospital and its routine. Originally, it had been for ex-servicemen, some of whom would be there for the remainder of their lives, but now it was open to all limbless people. Also it dealt with a number of surgical cases: six of the beds in my ward were reserved for this type of patient.

The routine was similar to that I had known at Welburn but it differed greatly in one respect: we had to be awake by six o'clock, even earlier if the ward was exceptionally busy. I never got accustomed to this, getting up early is not a good point with me.

Breakfast was at eight o'clock but there was a great deal of work to be completed in those two hours. After breakfast the patients who needed training to walk, would make their way to an adjoining hut. They returned to the ward at midday for lunch, then did about two hours more training. They were free in the evenings to watch TV – there was a set in each ward – or to amuse themselves until lights out at ten o'clock. One evening a week there was a film show in the recreation room. It was there, too, that a short service was held on Sunday mornings, for those of the Church of England denomination. Alternative arrangements were made for followers of other religions.

The following morning I began my "schooling", as the training sessions for the disabled were called. These sessions took place in a room with large mirrors at the end and what looked like parallel bars, but so low that one could walk between them, holding on to the bars for balance.

Vera Morris was the physiotherapist who trained the women. She was in her mid-thirties, a slimly built woman, with light brown hair and fair skin which was liberally covered with freckles.

A Mr Chilton was senior in rank to both her and the male instructor. He was of muscular build with a tanned complexion and dark hair, a quiet-spoken, reserved man in his forties.

It was Mr Chilton who wheeled me down a steep concrete slope to the Centre where I was to try on my equipment. It was comforting to be greeted by familiar faces and to be in surroundings that I knew.

Frank took us into the main fitting room where my leg

stood propped up against the wall. I am not sure what I had expected to see, but it was certainly not what was there. Quite frankly, I was dismayed. But I remembered that Douglas Bader had told me not to worry about how the leg looked.

The leg itself was unpainted, it looked shiny and new and was covered in little rivets, nuts and screws; dangling from it were buckles and laces. Beside it stood a sturdy looking black leather boot with a short caliper clipped into holes each side of the heel. This was added support for my right leg.

Before I had recovered from the initial shock, Frank had begun to fit the apparatus on to me. He slipped a short woolly "sock" over my left thigh and then he slid my leg into the artificial one. The lower half looked like tin with a black rubber pad at the bottom instead of a foot. Above the calf, metal bars came up on each side and were hinged at the knee for when I was sitting down. Between these bars was a soft leather bootee into which my own foot was firmly laced.

Next a leather corset was fastened around my thigh with two straps as well as laces. This in turn was attached to a wide belt which was laced tightly around my lower abdomen: Mr Chilton had to support me while I stood up for the completion of this tricky manoeuvre. Finally came the boot and caliper for my other leg.

During the time this had taken, my dismay had increased. The leather felt strange and uncomfortable against my skin and the whole thing felt heavy and cumbersome.

In time I grew accustomed to the weight but the restrictions were always irksome. When wearing the apparatus I was unable to do anything, it was even impossible to sit in an ordinary chair. By sitting forward in my wheelchair I was reasonably comfortable, if I sat further back it was the back of the chair which kept me upright and then the belt cut into my stomach.

The leg was supposed to enable me to lead a more normal life, but it seemed to me then that it was doing the very opposite. For the first time in my life I felt handicapped.

8
Success . . .

My training began with me learning to stand alone. This proved more difficult than any of us had anticipated, it was a matter of weeks rather than days before my balance was fairly stable. The situation was not helped by my fear of falling.

The procedure was for Vera Morris to stand me between the wall and my wheelchair so that I could not topple far either way. Gradually the gap between me and the chair was widened, also the length of time I stood there was increased as my leg grew stronger.

Eventually my balance was perfected to the satisfaction of Mr Thomson and my instructors. At last I had made some progress although I still felt that a puff of wind would knock me over. That was why I liked to have someone within easy reach of me.

During those weeks I had settled down to hospital life. With the constant change-over of patients there was always something to interest me, I gained an insight into many different facets of life. It all helped to dispel my feelings of being homesick.

The other patients were wonderful about sharing their visitors with me, but it's not the same as having someone of your own. My parents came up one weekend about a month

after I was admitted to Chapel Allerton. The visiting regula-
tions were relaxed for us but, even so, they were only able
to spend a limited time with me which hardly seemed to
make their long journey worthwhile.

The solution was for us all to spend an occasional weekend with our relatives at Moss. They readily agreed to the
plan and Mr Thomson was always happy to sign my weekend pass. On these occasions my Uncle Herbert would
collect me from the hospital late on the Friday afternoon,
then he would drive me back on the Sunday evening, after
my family had returned to Norfolk.

These precious weekends gave my family the opportunity to hear all my news, as alas, I had not improved at
letter-writing. And it was nice to have a break from hospital routine and be able to enjoy more freedom, even if
it was only for a few short hours.

But in between these visits I was lucky in having Margaret. Together with a friend she regularly visited some of
the permanent residents at the hospital. I was introduced
to her by two of the war disabled, Johnny and Wilf, after
which I was included in her visits.

Margaret, who was then in her twenties, was a sweet-
natured person. She had an attractive elfin like face, this
impression was heightened by her dark hair which she wore
shaped to her head. She has since become Mrs Trevor Burke
and is the mother of five small children, but even so she still
finds time to write me long, newsy letters.

Obviously a hospital is not geared to entertain a lively
teenager, so the time seemed long on Saturdays and Sundays
when we had no training. Apart from watching TV, the
only other recreations were playing cards or reading.

The library trolley was brought round every week which

was fortunate as I had an insatiable appetite for reading. The lady who did this voluntarily seemed to feel it was her duty to censor my choice of books. It was amusing how rigorously she carried this out; though it was not the success she believed because I found an ally in Vera Morris. She would sometimes borrow a banned book for me. I am sure that same, well-meaning trolley lady would have been shocked had she seen me playing solo whist.

I understood that Mr Williams made several enquiries about my progress. It was becoming increasingly obvious to me that it would be quite a while before I returned to Welburn.

The staff at Chapel Allerton were always extremely kind to me. They encouraged me to discuss any problems with them; although I am one of those people who keep things to themselves, it was comforting to know that I could talk with them if I wanted to. Also they made my life as interesting and varied as possible.

One of the nurses in Ward H, Nurse Adams, arranged a special treat for me. She arranged to take me to a matinee performance at a nearby cinema. Matron's permission was obtained before Nurse mentioned the outing to me, then she told me that it was to be on the coming Saturday, which was her day off.

I passed an anxious morning as it was pouring with rain and I knew the outing depended on fine weather. But by the afternoon the rain had eased to a heavy drizzle. To my relief Nurse Adams, a well-built woman of about forty, duly arrived carrying mackintoshes and an umbrella. After wrapping me up in these we set off. The cinema was only a few yards from the hospital entrance.

We entered the cinema through a side door and were

shown to our seats. I was able to remain in my wheelchair, as several of the tip-up seats had been removed from one corner for this purpose. Such a simple thing as that can make all the difference to the enjoyment of an outing for a disabled person. True, more places of entertainment are now copying this idea, but they are still a minority.

The film was "The Tommy Steele Story". I thoroughly enjoyed it but I am not so certain whether Nurse Adams did or not. She sat with her eyes closed for much of the time; though she assured me, afterwards, that she had only been resting her eyes, I was not absolutely convinced.

Nurse Adams also took me out on another excursion; it was when the Queen and the Duke of Edinburgh were on a visit to Leeds. One evening they attended a performance at the Opera House, passing Chapel Allerton en route from Harewood House. Knowing of my interest in the Royal Family, Nurse promised to take me to watch the procession go by.

We joined the crowds on the pavement outside our main gates several minutes before the Queen's car was due. We had not bothered to ask for Matron's consent for me to leave the hospital grounds, so there were a few anxious moments when she approached us. However, we need not have worried as she completely ignored the fact in her good humour.

A kindly young policeman guided us through to the front of the crowd so that I had an excellent view. Then we waited expectantly for the cars to appear.

The first indication of the approaching procession came from the cheers of the people farther along the road. Then we saw the police motor-cycles as they came around the corner, following them came the cars with their interiors brightly illuminated.

The Queen looked radiant in her evening gown and glittering jewels. At her side was the handsome figure of the Duke of Edinburgh, both of them were smiling and waving.

In the second car were Lord Harewood and his first wife, Marion, Lady Harewood. Her beauty was of a darker type than the Queen's but it was none the less for that.

Several more cars followed carrying other house-guests and members of the Royal household. But all too soon it was over and we returned to the more mundane routine of hospital life.

My training then consisted of walking around with Mrs Morris or Mr Chilton. I still needed their arm to support me because no matter how hard I tried I simply could not manage to take a step alone. As soon as I attempted to take my full weight on my left leg, I lost my balance, completely. My instructors assured me that things would be all right, given time. Frank pointed out that for nearly fifteen years my brain had not had to send out the signals telling me to walk, now suddenly it was expected to correct this. He seemed to believe that with patience and perseverance the brain would eventually co-operate.

I was aware of having the peculiar sensation of wearing my artificial leg, when in actual fact I was not. I had to be extremely careful on those occasions, so that if I stood up for any reason – perhaps to look out of a window – I did not attempt to put my weight on to my left leg.

Any slight change in my shape as my muscles hardened, resulted in adjustments having to be made to my artificial leg. A constant check was made on both my height and was with those of a quiet nature but I soon learned to stand on my own two feet + mix with everybody.

It was while I was at Wellburn that I was cured of my temper. I was storming away one day (I cannot recollect why) when I suddenly noticed the shocked faces of my friends. I resolved there + then never to fly into a rage again + I have kept to my word. Fortunately I retained enough spirit to hold my own in a discussion + I can fight my own battles!

The members of my class were studying for their "O" levels + so for a while I worked alone. I joined the others for biology which I was always interested in. I did Latin which I loathed with one other girl, Pauline Rogers, a frail looking girl with a sweet smile.

I think it is worth mentioning here that Mervyn White had told me that I had a talent for essay-writing, but Mr. Williams held the opposite view. I missed the freedom we had in choice

A sample page of the manuscript of *On My Toes*,
as received by the Publisher

weight, my height changed very slowly and finally came to a complete standstill when I reached a mere four feet. But alas, I gained weight rapidly.

I suppose it was inevitable, because apart from my training I was getting hardly any exercise. I was not even feeding myself. It was impossible for me to manage this when I was wearing my equipment, but despite my protests the nurses insisted on feeding me at other times too. I know their intentions were well-meaning but it did not help my weight problem. As my weight increased my mobility lessened, although I did regain some of it in due course the loss of mobility was never fully rectified.

I now used one of the hospital wheelchairs instead of my own, Ministry-issued one. The hospital model had large self-propelling wheels at the front, these enabled me to manoeuvre myself around the grounds by turning each wheel in turn with my right foot.

I was stupidly trying to manipulate the chair one day while I was wearing my apparatus. Suddenly my boot slipped off the wheel and with a sickening crunch I twisted my knee. The joint was painfully stiff for a week so I had an enforced, but not unwelcome rest, from my training. Unfortunately the injury was a recurring one which troubled me from time to time.

I was also having problems of a very different kind, but ones that are common to any adolescent. I was suffering the agonies of being in love – or so I thought. I had experienced the usual schoolgirl crushes but I had never before felt the attraction of a man.

Doubtless he had set many other female hearts fluttering, his considerable charm, coupled with his good looks, were quite a combination. He was a broad-shouldered man of about forty, with black crinkly hair and deep blue eyes. He must have known of my feelings for him but he never teased me as some men would have done, he always treated me with tact and gentle understanding.

But at fourteen one can be extremely fickle. Yet there is something special about the first stirrings of adult emotion that can never be forgotten, no matter how deep a love is experienced in the future.

I made no headway whatsoever with my walking. I wanted to discuss the situation with Mr Thomson but I could never do so as I found him rather an awesome figure. I suppose this was rather silly of me, he was a kind man if rather serious. But he had a sense of humour as the following incident shows.

I should explain that another patient and myself amused ourselves by picking the winners at the various race meetings each day. We had a high rate of success and would have made a nice profit if we had put money on our hunches.

Anyway on the afternoon in question Mr Thomson was about to leave after making his weekly round when he reached the door, paused, and turned back into the room. He smilingly asked me, "Are you as successful at doing the football coupons as you are at picking horses?"

It was one of those rare occasions in my life that I have been speechless. Exactly how Mr Thomson learned of our pastime remains a mystery.

Eventually the day came when I managed to take my first steps without help. True, I only managed three precarious ones before someone had to steady me but at last all the effort and waiting seemed worthwhile.

9
. . . and Failure

My success was short-lived. Apart from managing a few steps at home during one of my holidays, I never walked again without a supporting arm.

I think I foresaw how the venture would end, at least a year before anyone else admitted that it had failed. During those intervening months various modifications were made to the leg. When I outgrew the first leg, the rubber pad at the bottom was replaced on the new one by a triangular shaped wooden "rocker" (this was later replaced by a proper foot).

Mr Thomson even suggested that artificial arms might help to improve my balance. A plaster cast was made of the entire upper half of my body, but then the idea was shelved.

My instructors would have been very surprised if they had known how little it bothered me when I first suspected that the experiment with the artificial leg was going to fail. But for me it only meant that I would be returning to the kind of life I had always known, and what was so terrible about that?

I did wonder how my family would feel as their hopes must have been high that the venture would succeed. But they, like me, had realised that success would create its own problems. The artificial leg made it impossible for me to even sit properly, then I could not do anything with my feet. So, if I had worn my leg for any length of time – as I would have done if I could have walked – then artificial arms would have been a necessity. The result would have been yet more weight and discomfort for me to contend with.

However, for the present my training continued much as usual. But it was surprisingly interrupted one afternoon with the news that I had visitors. While Mrs Morris removed my equipment I wondered about their identity, but I was no nearer the solution when I was wheeled into one of the side wards. Then I saw the smiling faces of Harold and Ivy Cooke which revived all my happy memories of Welburn.

But the summer of 1958 was to bring an even greater surprise for me. The first indication I had of this was just a few days before I was due to begin my summer holiday. Then Mr Chilton told me that I would be going home a day earlier than had been originally planned. Beyond that he refused to tell me any more. Though I was puzzled I certainly had no objections as it meant an extra day at home. I was sure that my mother would explain the reason for the change of date as soon as she arrived at Chapel Allerton. However, explanations were left until we reached home then my mother showed me a letter. It was headed "Central Fighter Establishment, R.A.F. West Raynham" and it read:

Dear Mrs. Smith,

Group Captain Bader has sent me your letter and has agreed to see your daughter whilst he is here on the 30th July.

I would like to suggest that you come to the Guardroom at the main entrance where I will arrange for someone to meet you and show you into my office where the Group Captain will see your daughter at 7.30 p.m.

Trusting that these arrangements will be convenient and with best wishes I am,

Yours sincerely,
R. B. Lord
(Wing Commander,
Officer Commanding)

Naturally I was thrilled at the prospect of actually meeting Douglas Bader the following evening. The intervening hours seemed interminable. But at last it was time for my parents and I to set off on the short journey to West Raynham. I was not very comfortable as I was wearing my artificial leg, so I was relieved when I saw the airfield in the distance.

The sentry on duty at the main gate was expecting us. He directed us to the Guardroom where we were handed over to a young R.A.F. policeman, who looked after us for the remainder of our visit.

Wing-Commander Lord conducted us to a small room where Douglas Bader was awaiting our arrival. The other officers withdrew discreetly, leaving us to have a few minutes private conversation with the Group-Captain.

I felt nervous but Douglas soon put me at my ease and then conversation flowed freely. We talked mainly about my apparatus and of my progress – such as it was – at Chapel Allerton. I recall saying that my leg had been made by Hangers, the manufacturers of his own legs.

I was greatly impressed by this stockily built man, who

stumped around the room as we talked. Beneath his friendliness one could sense his iron hard determination which had enabled him to conquer seemingly insurmountable odds.

When we were rejoined by the station personnel, Wing-Commander Lord was carrying a book in his hand, which he then presented to me. It was a copy of Douglas Bader's biography, *Reach For The Sky* by Paul Brickhill. The inscription on the fly-leaf read:

"Happy days Maureen. Douglas Bader 30/7/58"

We were given a welcome cup of strong R.A.F. tea in an ante-room. Then our police escort took us to the part of the station where Group-Captain Bader, now accompanied by his late wife Thelma, was to open the fête which was the reason for his visit to Norfolk. But for me, the most memorable part of the evening was over.

On my return to Chapel Allerton I found that one of my fellow patients, Mrs Jackson, never tired of hearing my account of that exciting meeting. She had been visited in hospital, some years before, by Douglas Bader.

"Jacko" was then in her early sixties. She had no close family; because of sugar diabetes she had lost both of her legs, as well as her eyesight. Her life had been dogged by tragedy, but she had remained cheerful and never complained. She was the most unselfish person I have ever known.

At about that time another nursing auxiliary began working at Chapel Allerton. She was Hazel Stonehouse, a tall, fair-haired young person with a happy, smiling face.

Hazel had only been married for a few months and she was proud of her husband Ian. It was some two years before I met him, by which time they had a daughter, Julie. We corresponded through the years, during which Hazel had three more children, including twin boys. We did not meet again until 1970, when we had a happy reunion, shortly before the Stonehouse family left England to begin a new life in Canada.

In the autumn of '58 we spent one of our regular family weekends at Moss. My cousin Hazel was only too willing to demonstrate her new acquisition, a portable typewriter. At my uncle's suggestion I tried to use the machine, I found that I could manage it without too much difficulty. Nevertheless, it was a great surprise when I saw that my parents had given me an identical model for my Christmas present.

It was impossible for me to touch type. I found that the best method was for me to use only the big toe of my right foot, I preferred this way to using sticks or some other aid. This "one finger exercise" was laboriously slow, even after much practice my maximum speed was only fifteen words a minute. None of the other operations in the use of the machine presented any difficulties. So at least I had the satisfaction of being able to type, however slowly.

I had begun experimenting with cosmetics and at first the results were disastrous. My mouth looked as if it had been daubed with plum jam. Also I used far too much foundation in an attempt to hide the angry-looking spots on my face, which only made the acne worse. But one learns by one's mistakes. I applied my make-up with my left foot using just the ordinary materials. I was able to manage without any special aids, although I did find a long-handled comb useful.

Unhappily my acne stayed a problem, despite a course

of treatment I underwent at the hands of "Robbie", a nursing auxiliary. Each night she would paint my spots with a foul-smelling, black paste. But it never made the slightest difference, nor have I out-grown it, not even now.

Changes were taking place in the hospital, due partly to the fact that we had a new Secretary. He had been a Colonel or something similar in the Army and seemed determined to run the hospital with military discipline. This made him most unpopular with the patients.

Perhaps things were not as bad as we thought. Until then we had been allowed more freedom than is customary in many hospitals. But the added restrictions were extremely irksome. It was the final straw, as far as I was concerned, when he refused to allow Hazel and Ian Stonehouse to take me to the cinema to see "Tiger Bay". After that, I felt I had had enough of hospital life for a time. All I really wanted to do was to return to my studies.

For quite some time I had been concerned about my loss of education. It was about eighteen months since I had last seen a school text book.

My anxiety was underlined by a letter I received one morning from Denis Browne. Although he had expressed his genuine interest whenever my mother sent him reports of my activities or photographs of me, this was the first time he had written to me.

In his letter, Denis Browne asked if I was interested in teaching handicapped children. If I wished to make a career of this, he offered to help me find a position in a special school.

I explained in my reply to Mr Browne, that my own education had been sadly neglected during my stay at Chapel Allerton. This had to be rectified before I could seek employment, however, when that time came I would give his kind offer my full consideration.

Only a few days before I was to begin my Easter holiday in 1959, I received an unexpected gentleman visitor. It was the headmaster from the school opposite the limb-fitting centre, which I knew was a day-school for physically handicapped children.

Apparently, after it became plain that my stay at Chapel Allerton would be a prolonged one, the Norfolk Education Authorities had instructed the Yorkshire people to provide me with some alternative method of tuition. It was only now that it had been realised that because of a misunderstanding nothing had been arranged. So, rather belatedly, the error was being corrected.

As it was not possible for me to have full-time tuition, three teachers, including the headmaster, agreed to teach me after normal school hours. They worked out a rota which was convenient to them and resulted in my lessons lasting for two hours each week-day. In addition, they set me work to do at weekends. Sister Lawson was most helpful in allowing us to use a side-ward.

Several weeks were spent on doing revision work but gradually we broke new ground. The subjects we concentrated on were English Language and Literature, History and Maths. Although the arrangement only lasted for one term it was a success.

While I was waiting down at the limb-centre one morning to have an alteration to my leg, Mr Thomson stopped to have a short chat with me. He remarked that it might improve my balance if my hip was "fixed". There was something almost too casual about the remark which disturbed me.

After lunch I wheeled myself along to the "walking school". I knew there was time for me to have a quiet talk with Mrs Morris before anyone interrupted us.

Mr Thomson had already mentioned this new move to his staff, but they had not expected him to mention it to me yet, if ever. They had hoped that he would decide against such action.

Vera Morris was perfectly frank with me. If the experiment failed in helping me to walk, then a stiff hip would only add to my disability. Even though it could succeed she strongly advised me against having any operation. But I had to make the final decision.

It did not take me long to decide. I felt that the risk was too great. I intended to make this abundantly clear to Mr Thomson the next time he raised the subject. Perhaps he had only been clutching at straws when he made the suggestion; I knew he never admitted defeat with a case or maybe someone else told him of my feelings, but whatever the reason the matter was not mentioned again.

While I was at home for my summer holiday we had a letter from Mr Thomson. On his way back to Leeds from a visit to London, he wished to make a detour to Gateley for a talk with my parents and myself.

The purpose of Mr Thomson's visit appeared to be to see how I felt about the idea that I should be transferred from Chapel Allerton to Roehampton. I was quite adamant that if I had to return to hospital then I would prefer it to be Chapel Allerton. At the end of his visit Mr Thomson once again affirmed his belief that I would walk.

Despite my feelings, an appointment was made for me to see a specialist at Roehampton. Because of special arrangements our journey was much easier than those previous ones, back in the days when I attended Great Ormond Street Hospital. A car took us to Norwich Thorpe Station from where our seats had been reserved on the train, a taxi awaited our arrival at Liverpool Street. The whole procedure was reversed for the return journey.

I had been told to take my artificial leg with me but the doctor I saw was more interested in fitting me with arms. The idea did not appeal to me – it was not until much later that I considered why this was – so I was not very forthcoming. Perhaps the doctor thought my reluctance was due to the unsuccessful period at Chapel Allerton. Anyhow he did not press his ideas too strongly.

When it became clear that I would not be returning to Chapel Allerton there were a few loose ends to tidy up. For instance I had to return the text books I had needed for the holiday work my teachers had given me. But still one problem remained. What was I to do now? It was a decision I could not put off for much longer.

10
New Horizons

The Fakenham Club for the Physically Handicapped was founded by the Red Cross in November 1958. It began under its chairman, Mrs Grace Wurr, with only eleven members. However, this number rapidly increased to a total of forty-five and it has remained more or less at that figure throughout the years.

Grace Wurr, an attractive person of small build who was then approaching middle-age, proved to be an ideal person for such a responsibility. Her two children, John and Margaret, were growing up fast and so she had more time for interests outside her home. Her boundless energy and genuine interest in other people were points in her favour too.

My association with the Club began when a woman in a Red Cross uniform knocked at our door. Though I did not know it at the time that woman was Grace Wurr.

There were only Bernard and I at home that morning as my mother worked part-time in those days. In answer to her enquiry, Bernard gave the stranger directions for finding my mother. And so it was not until lunch-time that we learned the identity of the caller or the reason for her visit.

Apparently Mrs Wurr had learned of my disability from her husband Ralph, who was an inspector for the Prudential Assurance Company. Immediately, she regarded me as a prospective member for the Club she ran: hence her visit.

Being uncertain of my reactions to the idea, my mother had not given Mrs Wurr a definite answer. However, she agreed to Mrs Wurr's suggestion that I should accompany the members on one of their outings, before I decided one way or the other.

Aunt Rene and Myra were staying with us that summer so they also went on the trip, which was a half-day's visit to the east coast resort of Hunstanton. It gave me the opportunity to renew my acquaintance with Jennifer Howe, the disabled girl who had been at Ryburgh School with me. It was a pleasant surprise to find that she was a member of the Club. That discovery got the afternoon off to a good start and although most of the other members were considerably older than me, I found them good company.

The outcome was that I became a member of the Club, though my plans for the future were still uncertain. It was a decision that made quite a difference to my life and one that I have never regretted.

The Club meetings were held monthly in the W.I. Hall at Fakenham: several years later we moved to the new Health Centre in the town and then fortnightly handicraft classes were begun.

Mrs Wurr was always willing to approach anyone, no matter who it was, for help whenever it was needed. It took a really hard heart to refuse her too, when she was exerting her not inconsiderable charm to its fullest extent.

But as the existence of the Club became more widely known Mrs Wurr's persuasive powers were needed less frequently. Offers of practical help came from many sources. Voluntary transport drivers were found; people in the district with large homes and gardens invited us to use them for our summer meetings; the Round Table became responsible for arranging the annual birthday party; finally, R.A.F. West Raynham accepted similar responsibility for a Christmas Party, whenever their duties allowed them sufficient time.

Other organisations, too numerous to mention, gave generous donations towards our general running expenses. In recent years their generosity has taken the tangible form of wheelchairs or other equipment.

I decided not to return to Welburn. I did not like the idea of being away from home again, so soon. Also, and this was the main reason for my decision, I was not ready, academically, to join the pupils of my age group who would be studying for their G.C.E. "O" level exams.

I was then faced with the dilemma of deciding which other course to adopt. I decided to wait a while before making any irrevocable decisions. In the meantime there were other problems to be resolved.

Marshall & Snelgrove had always made my capes but they were unable to continue this kind of service any longer. And now that I was older, ready-made articles of clothing, such as dresses, needed considerable alteration before they fitted me satisfactorily.

The obvious solution to both those problems was to find a good dressmaker. It proved much more difficult than we had anticipated but eventually we succeeded. Regrettably, after a while, her husband's job took them away from the district. Since then I have had a succession of dressmakers: as soon as I find a new one something happens so that she has to give up the work.

Another difficulty was in finding a hairdresser, as all the

ladies hair saloons in our area seemed to occupy first-floor premises. Mrs Noy helped here by giving us the name of her own hairdresser, Janet Woodcock, who ran a business at her home. This highly satisfactory arrangement was a permanent solution and we soon came to regard Mrs Woodcock as a friend.

In an attempt to become as independent as possible, I approached the Ministry about being issued with some kind of self-propelling vehicle. I had to attend Norfolk House, the artificial limb and appliance centre in Norwich, for a medical. It was then left to the engineers to decide which model could best be adapted to suit my needs.

The machine that was finally delivered to my home was unbelievable: it looked like something that might have been in Noah's Ark. It was a large, upright contraption with no protection from the weather, there was something vaguely reminiscent of an early motor car about it. It was not self-propelling but had to be operated by someone walking behind it, and because the machine was battery-powered the operator had to have a driving licence. Its slowest speed, 5 m.p.h., was too fast a pace for the "walker" to maintain over any distance.

The vehicle was virtually useless so after only a few weeks we returned it to the Ministry. I tried again but to no avail. I simply could not convince the engineers that they could design a suitable vehicle for me without much difficulty. So in the end I agreed to accept an ordinary wheelchair. If only those engineers would learn to be more flexible in their attitude to adapting standard equipment, then it would be easier for a disabled person to take an active part in the community.

But to some extent, I did achieve financial independence

at about that time. Independence of any kind is most important to a disabled person but, probably, this is even more so when it comes to financial independence.

We had discussed amongst ourselves the possibility of my receiving Social Security benefit—or National Assistance as it was then known. My father was certain that I would not be able to get the allowance, but we intended to try for it, anyway. We did not see about it immediately as we believed that I was still under age.

Then one of those strange coincidences of life occurred. A Welfare Officer from East Dereham, Mr Boothman, came to see me on the same matter. He helped us complete all the formalities and in due course I received my first allowance book.

It was now almost nine months since I had returned home. A decision about my future had to be made without further delay.

It was while I was glancing through the advertisements in the newspaper one day, that I had the idea for taking a Correspondence Course. Being uncertain of which of the Correspondence Schools to approach, I wrote to Dr Lincoln Ralphs for some advice.

I was doing some weeding in the front garden a few days later, when a car stopped at the gate. The man who stepped out of the car was of small build, with straight hair which was greying, as also was his neatly trimmed moustache.

After ascertaining that he was at the correct address, the stranger introduced himself. It was not until we had gone into the house to talk, that I learned why Frank Lawson, the maths teacher at Fakenham Grammar School, had come to see me.

Apparently Dr Ralphs had contacted the headmaster at Fakenham, as he felt that in addition to taking a Correspondence Course I would benefit from having some personal tuition. As he was willing to take on the rôle of my tutor, Mr Lawson had come to discuss the necessary arrangements with me.

I wished to take three "O" levels—English Language, English Literature and Mathematics. Frank Lawson suggested that I should prepare to take the exams in the summer of 1962. As it was then April 1960 we had slightly more than two years in which to complete five years' work.

My lessons were three evenings a week for a total of six hours. It was a similar routine to the two previous occasions I had received tuition outside normal school hours. During the day I completed the work set me by the Correspondence School.

Mr Lawson and I had an excellent teacher-pupil relationship which enabled us to work well together. He was most conscientious about his work, if he ever missed a lesson then he made it up another time. But those were rare occasions, even when winter road conditions were extremely hazardous.

Shortly after I became a member of the disabled club I was introduced to Susie Peachment. Susie, who was then twenty-seven, was a tall, well-built person with fair hair. She had been born with an arthritic leg and the disease had steadily progressed through the years. She had also lost her eyesight only a short while after her marriage in 1953.

It was at Susie's suggestion that we both joined a party of our fellow members on a specially organised holiday.

These special holidays for the disabled and elderly, were held at Gorleston Holiday Camp—near Great Yarmouth—after their season had ended. As the demand for this type of holiday increased, so other local camps followed Gorleston's example.

Susie and I enjoyed ourselves so much that that holiday was the first of many. The entertainment programme was full and varied, and the food was excellent. The staff and management did everything in their power to make our week's stay as happy and comfortable as possible.

Each group of disabled campers was accompanied by their families or other able-bodied helpers. As Grace Wurr felt that this should be an opportunity for our families to have a break, she and at least one other person travelled with the Fakenham party. Any additional assistance that was needed came from the "free-lance" helpers. The "free-lancers" consisted mainly of students. They were always willing to participate in shopping expeditions or late-night walks along the promenade.

I can recall a party that Susie and I held in our chalet one evening, for some of the students who had been particularly helpful to our group. As the hour grew late the conversation amongst our assorted company was deep and serious. We were all so engrossed that the party did not break-up until 2 a.m.

In the summer of 1961, Mrs Wurr asked me to form an Entertainment Group, within the Club. As its activities expanded I became so deeply involved with the running of the Group, that I have decided to devote a later chapter to this alone.

With only a few weeks remaining before the exams began, I took an evening off from my studies. My family took me to Great Yarmouth to see Bruce Forsyth, who was doing a summer season there that year.

We waited to see the artistes leave the theatre, after the show. The supporting acts, including the late Gary Miller – he stopped to give me his autograph – left first. Then came Bruce.

He immediately came over to speak to me. He was very kind and stood chatting several minutes before moving off to sign his autograph for some more people. A man carrying an armful of bronze and yellow chrysanthemums had joined the crowd in the meantime. Bruce gave the flowers to me, explaining at the same time that the gentleman wished me to have them. Where the stranger or his flowers came from, I never knew. But I have never forgotten his kind gesture which was the perfect ending to a memorable evening.

With only a few days remaining before the exams began, I received final confirmation of the arrangements made, enabling me to take them in my own home.

My invigilator was Brenda Russell, whose husband had succeeded Mervyn White as the headmaster at Ryburgh school. In addition to being responsible for sending each completed paper to its respective "marker", Mrs Russell was also to assist me with any accurate Geometry constructions. Because she would be acting under my precise instructions, Brenda Russell was allowed to have one practice session with me. One other concession was made, I was given extra time in which to complete the essay paper. I was pleased that I did not need to use any of it because, as far as possible, I wanted to work under identical conditions to the other candidates.

The exams did not present any major difficulties and so

I felt confident about the results: perhaps too confident.
The results were to be announced in September and until
then there was nothing to do, except wait.

II
Meeting the Press

Those two months of waiting passed by quite quickly. I was able to catch up on my reading and all the little chores I had neglected because of the pressure of school-work.

Also I frequently spent a day in Fakenham, mostly either at the home of Mrs Wurr or Susie Peachment, but sometimes I would visit Mrs Dennis who was also a helper at the disabled club.

As I came to know Mrs Wurr better I realised just how involved she was with the members of the club. If she knew that any of them needed help, perhaps in time of family illness, she was soon knocking at their door. At times it almost seemed as if her own family had to take second place. It was a great credit to them that they accepted this with such forbearance and were never heard to complain.

Grace Wurr's personal involvement with me began when she took me along with her to functions at the local Grammar School, where her daughter Margaret was a pupil.

I was always welcomed on these occasions by both staff and pupils alike. The headmaster, Mr Eckersley, always made an enquiry about the progress of my studies. It was good to be made to feel a part of the school community.

It was through Mrs Wurr that I began painting. My tutor was Mr Willis, a retired schoolmaster who was secretary for the disabled club. Sadly my lessons were halted by Mr Willis' death, after only a few short months. I had enjoyed working under his tuition but I knew I had no real talent for painting, and so I never bothered to find another instructor.

I also gave much consideration that summer to choosing a suitable career. It was then that I thought about Denis Browne's offer to help me find a post if I wished to teach handicapped children. It was an attractive proposition but one that I rejected for two reasons. It would mean spending a good deal of time away from home which did not appeal to me. And, much as I love children, I was not convinced that I wanted to spend my life teaching them.

Probably because of having spent long periods in hospital, I was keenly interested in anything connected with the medical profession. But that type of work was not practically possible.

At last I decided to take Mr Lawson's advice and become a writer. It was something I could do without my disability causing any practical difficulties. Whether Frank Lawson was correct in his belief that I had a talent for writing still had to be proved, or disproved, whichever the case may be. But I knew that I had a good imagination and most important of all, I enjoyed writing. The more I thought about the idea, the more I liked it. But Fate was not yet ready for me to embark on such a project, as I soon discovered.

I was most surprised when, on the morning of September 5th, my mother returned home, after having left for work only a short time before.

"What's wrong?" I enquired anxiously.

"Nothing," my mother assured me, "but Mr Lawson

has just telephoned Mrs Rivett. He has the results of your exams."

I waited with bated breath.

She continued, "You have passed in English Language but not in Literature or Maths. Mr Lawson is coming out later this morning to see you about taking them again."

I was bitterly disappointed, but I tried to conceal this fact from my mother as she was so pleased about my single success. Then, when she returned to work, I was left alone with my thoughts until Mr Lawson arrived.

I was upset by the thought that I had failed so many people, particularly Frank Lawson. I felt that I owed him some kind of apology for failing Maths, which was his subject. I was determined to do better at the next attempt.

Mr Lawson seemed relieved to hear that there was going to be a "next time". But I never once considered ending my studies at such an unsatisfactory stage, failure usually spurs me on to greater efforts.

My disappointment at my moderate success was quickly dispelled by the exciting events of the next few days.

It began the following day when, while reading our local newspaper, *The Eastern Daily Press*, I spotted an item referring to my exam results. I was mystified as to how the Press had acquired the information: I still am. I know that a reporter contacted Mr Lawson by telephone but, typically, he did not disclose his original source of information.

The report only ran to a couple of paragraphs but it started the snowball rolling. I had hardly finished reading it when, through the living-room window, I saw two men walking up the garden path. It was obvious from the equipment he was carrying that one of the men was a photographer. I learned that the other was Tony Scase, an interviewer well-known to listeners of radio's "Today" programme. As well as working for the BBC, Tony did freelance Press work.

I was most surprised when Tony Scase explained that he wished to interview me for the national papers. I could not really understand why my one "O" level was causing so much interest. Nevertheless it was all rather thrilling and as the interview proceeded I found myself enjoying it.

Then it was the photographer's turn. He expected that one of the photographs would be used on TV that evening, in the regional news bulletin. (Because of Tony Scase's association with the BBC, we broke a long-standing habit that evening and watched the regional news on BBC instead of on ITV. Was the photograph of me shown? Oh yes— on ITV!)

The photographic session was ended. While the lights were being dismantled and packed away, Tony Scase went to telephone someone at the BBC. He returned with the exciting news that he had been given the "go-ahead" to interview me for the "Today" programme. A shortened version would be included on a later programme, "Friday Review".

After working out a list of questions from the information I had given him previously, Tony went through them with me before he began the actual recording.

As he packed away the tape-recorder afterwards, Tony remarked that if a more important item of news came in, then my item would be omitted from the programmes. After that, there was no danger of my ego being over-inflated. Fate was on my side though and the interview with me was broadcast. It was nice too, to receive a cheque from the BBC for 5 gns., as the payment for my contribution. Also, they gave me a copy of the recording as a souvenir.

The reaction to my publicity was totally unexpected. I received cards and letters from literally all over the British Isles. I was deeply touched by the kindness of all those people, many of whom were complete strangers.

From those many greetings I would like to single out just two for special mention. One was from Geoffrey Trease, the author, together with a copy of his book of practical advice to "The Young Writer".

The second letter was from Dr James Leckie of Aberdeen. Dr Leckie was directly responsible for my friendship with Marilyn Gillies. Marilyn had been born some twenty-one years before, without arms. She now worked as a typist in her home town of Dundee. Although Marilyn was more mobile than me – her legs were perfectly normal – Dr Leckie was sure that we would both benefit from an exchange of views.

Gradually the excitement quietened down and I was able to return to my studies. Dr Ralphs was agreeable that my lessons with Mr Lawson should continue on the same basis as before. He agreed too that the services of the Correspondence School were not really needed.

Frank Lawson felt that it would be better if some way could be found so that I could manage to do any Geometry constructions myself. He was certain that it would then be much easier for me to remember the steps used in the constructions, and also might save valuable time during the exam.

Mr Lawson was good at making things and after much thought he designed and made instruments which I could use unaided. They consisted of a standard pair of compasses which were adapted slightly to meet my requirements, and a special ruler.

The ruler was a thick piece of wood which Mr Lawson had shaped and polished, it was weighted so that it did not slide about. On the top was a plastic knob so that I could lift it easily. I used this ruler solely for drawing straight lines, when taking exact measurements I used my adapted compasses and an ordinary ruler. I had two of these attached to a thick board which in turn was screwed to the table I used when studying.

After practising for a while with these aids I was able to manage them satisfactorily. Not only did they enable me to do constructions without someone else helping me, but I began to like my work more.

For some time discussions had been taking place about modernising our cottage and the one adjoining it. Various schemes were suggested as to the best way of doing this. The course finally decided on was to rehouse the family in the other cottage, then to convert the two into one house.

The first stage – the rehousing of our neighbours – had been accomplished. I had not realised how this would help me but, with my mother working in the mornings, I was now able to study for a few hours without fear of interruption. In actual fact it was more than a year before my peace was shattered by the noise of builders at work.

In the intervening months numerous difficulties were encountered. Letters passed between the people concerned and the various Government departments but it seemed impossible to get a unanimous verdict on anything. By the summer of 1962 negotiations had reached a complete deadlock. It was at that critical point that I became directly involved.

I wrote to our local M.P., Albert Hilton – later Lord Hilton of Upton – asking for his help. After coming to see the situation for himself Mr Hilton promised to see if the Minister would personally intervene.

The Minister's reply duly came: he could do nothing.

Fortunately for us Mr Rivett was not easily deterred. After two years of negotiations he achieved the necessary breakthrough, the builders began work. Even then things did not always go smoothly but progress with the modernisation was made slowly.

1963 was a year of happiness and sadness.

On March 16th our dear friend Molly Pearce died suddenly. Her death was a great loss to us all, it was one we still feel today.

But life goes on. And on April 26th my first godchild was born. Margaret was the eldest daughter of Derek and Elaine Clark who lived at Gayton. Once again I was godmother when a daughter, Mandy Jane, was born to my cousin Betty and her husband Alan on July 10th. These two events gave me great pleasure as I have always been very fond of children.

We went to North Wales that summer for our family holiday. It was while we were there that I realised a personal ambition by meeting the popular pianist, Russ Conway. It was a meeting that so nearly did not take place, that it did was due entirely to the kind consideration Russ has for his fans.

I had been an admirer of Russ for some time and a member of his official Fan Club since it began some three years previously. So when I learned that he was doing a

summer season that year at Llandudno we arranged to
see the show one evening, together with Aunt Rene and
Myra. When we collected the tickets from the box-office
the previous afternoon, I handed in a letter for Russ in
which I made a request to meet him after the show.

As we left the theatre the following evening I asked
the elderly commissionaire to direct us to the stage-door.
In answer to my full explanation of why we wanted to
wait there, he assured us that there was no possibility of
seeing Russ. But he offered to get his autograph for me if
I cared to leave my autograph book.

Myra and I were particularly disappointed at not meeting Russ. However, we were determined not to let it spoil
our previous enjoyment of the show.

When we collected my autograph book the next day we
found a most agitated commissionaire. Shortly after we
had left the theatre the previous evening, Russ had come
to the stage-door as I had requested. (A letter telling me
this was awaiting me when we returned home.) Most artistes
would have left it at that but not Russ. He gave instructions that he was to be informed, if he was at the theatre,
when I returned for my autograph book.

The first house was about to commence, but Russ sent
out a message that he would see me if we waited until he
came off stage after the short opening act.

About five minutes later the door opened at the top of
a flight of steps and Russ appeared. He was wearing a
maroon suit and carrying a lighted cigarette in his left hand.
His face was "tanned" with stage make-up. We found him
a most charming person although he appeared to be rather
shy.

Russ stayed talking for several minutes, then he had to

leave us to change in readiness for his next appearance on stage. But we met again, it was some four years later when he was doing a series of Sunday concerts at Great Yarmouth.

During our meeting at Llandudno I had been vaguely conscious of a by-stander taking photographs. But, to my regret, I never thought about arranging to receive copies until it was much too late. It would have been nice to have a tangible memento of the occasion.

The date of my exams was drawing near. We had originally intended that I should take them that summer, but because of a misunderstanding over the final entrance date I was having to wait until the autumn.

Brenda Russell was again my invigilator. For my second attempt I was not allowed any special concessions which pleased me. By then I was well used to handling the geometry instruments Mr Lawson had made for me.

There were only two papers for me to take so it was soon over. All I had to do then was to wait for the results and about those I was far from being confident.

At this point in my story I would like to pause for a while, as I promised, to recount more fully the work undertaken by that branch of the Fakenham Club for the Physically Handicapped, known as the Entertainment Group.

12
The Entertainment Group

It was in June 1961 that Grace Wurr approached me about forming an Entertainment Group with Susie Peachment and Jennifer Howe. The purpose for such a Group was that it should provide the entertainment at club meetings for which there was no guest speaker.

Both Susie and Jennifer had pleasant singing voices but why Mrs Wurr considered me suitable to head such a project I cannot imagine. It was something though that I thoroughly enjoyed, particularly after I began to contribute with monologues or by teaming up with Susie to do short sketches. It reminded me of those happy days at Ryburgh Primary School when I had produced those end-of-term plays.

Rather surprisingly we began to receive invitations to entertain at other social clubs, by the autumn we were doing this, literally, all over the county. It was most gratifying to see the pleasure we gave our audiences, whether they be young or old. Also we were proving something that we fervently believed in, that, given the opportunity, the disabled can make a valuable contribution to society.

Tangible proof of our success was received when we won the talent competition at a rally for disabled clubs which was held at Saffron Walden. The trophy, a silver cup, was borne proudly back to Fakenham. I doubt if a happier trio than Susie, Jennifer and I, could have been found anywhere in Norfolk that evening.

It was at about the same time that we began to consider the idea of helping to increase club funds by our becoming a fund-raising Committee. Sadly, Jennifer decided that she was unsuited to this type of work, but she promised to give us her support in a non-administrative rôle. The idea met with the approval of Grace Wurr and our Red Cross helpers. They assured Susie and me of their willingness to give us any physical assistance that we might need, and this they always did, acting under our instructions and never interfering with our plans. And so we went ahead with Susie being the ideas "man" while I coped with all the secretarial work involved, in addition to my duties as chairman.

Our reasons for making this change were quite simple. We were limited by our disabilities to the type of material we could use. Also we could not rely indefinitely on outside "bookings" and after such a fine start it would be a pity for the Group to fade into obscurity.

Our new project got off to an ambitious start when Susie suggested that we produce a variety show. After careful consideration we both felt that it was a feasible proposition, but there followed hours of planning before we committed ourselves by taking any positive action.

The first people I contacted were the management of the Central Cinema in Fakenham. Though it meant that we would have to hire a stage, the cinema seemed an ideal venue as regards seating arrangements. Not only did the management agree to our using their premises but on that occasion they waived any hire charge. Their only condition was that the show would have to be on a Sunday afternoon so as not to interfere with their usual performances.

Before we proceeded any further we checked with the police on the Sunday entertainment laws. Apart from the possibility of prosecution by the Lord's Day Observance Society (here we trusted to Providence), there was one major difficulty – we were not allowed to charge an admission fee. On hearing this we had visions of having to cancel the whole idea as our sole aim was to make money. But the police were able to help us find a solution to the problem without us breaking any laws. Admission could be by pro- gramme only and they could be sold prior to the event. Programmes offered another source of revenue too, adver- tising space to be bought by local traders.

That was the first of our many problems resolved. We were then able to confirm the date for the show: Sunday, May 20th.

The next item on the agenda was to "book" the artistes who would take part in the show. We set a high standard when selecting the acts because we wanted the concert to be as professional as possible. At the same time the acts had to combine to make a well-varied programme of enter- tainment. This proved much easier than we had expected and we had soon compiled a list of the following acts:

The Blue Notes, a children's choir from the U.S.A.F. base at Sculthorpe; The Electrons, a group from Fakenham whose style was similar to that of The Shadows; Walter Hutton, a disabled vocalist from Norwich; Jean Rowe, our second vocalist; The Swanees, a Harmonica Trio all of whom were confined to wheelchairs; Johnny Tew, who was then the entertainments manager at Gorleston Holiday Camp – Johnny's speciality was comedy in mime. The live acts were completed by Susie and myself with George Challice as accompanist on the electric organ.

In 1960, the Norfolk Association for the Care of the Handicapped had made a film of the disabled on holiday at Gorleston. We hired the film to be shown in the spot immediately preceding the interval.

Long before then Susie and I had realised the value of having a celebrity as compère, but all our efforts to procure one had failed. However, not all of my letters had fallen on barren ground, Russ Conway offered us an autographed L.P. as a Lucky Programme Number prize. (I was pleased to have the opportunity to thank him personally when we met in Llandudno later in the year.)

Time was running out. But shortly before the programmes went to print the difficulty over a celebrity compère was resolved. Susie succeeded in booking Colin Bower (he was working at that time for Anglia, our local ITV network) for a fee of twenty-five guineas, though on the day of the show he kindly told us we could forget his fee.

I have only mentioned some of the more important aspects of the venture but we also had a number of smaller details to settle. These involved seeing to the hiring of the stage and other equipment, and planning the menu for the tea we were giving for our fellow artistes and club members. At last all the arrangements were completed that could be before the Great Day itself.

May 20th dawned bright and sunny. It was already pleasantly warm when, immediately after breakfast, my family and I left home for Fakenham, to help with the final preparations.

Susie and I spent most of the morning at the W.I. Hall, where our lady helpers were busy preparing the food and arranging the tables in readiness for the meal we were having after the show had ended. When they had finished we walked the few yards from the Hall to the cinema, to see how the menfolk were progressing with the arrangements there.

Our decision to leave the men to their own devices had been a wise one. They had encountered a number of problems which we had been unable to foresee, even though we had gone over every detail many times during those five months of planning. By the time we arrived on the scene they had succeeded in erecting the stage but there were still the drapes and curtains to be hung.

With less than an hour left before the curtain was due to go up, the final details were completed. That we were ready in time was thanks to all those kind people who forfeited their Sunday morning to help us.

I doubt if we would have had any lunch that day had it not been that we had arranged to stay in town at Susie's home. Even so it was a hectic time, with about a dozen people all trying to get ready at once, we kept meeting outside the bathroom door in various stages of undress. It was long past the time we should have been there to welcome the artistes when we did eventually leave on the short journey to the cinema.

As we hurried inside it was comforting to see a long queue waiting for the doors to open. Although we had sold several hundred programmes there was no way of knowing how many people would actually come to see us. (We need not have worried as there was a full capacity house for the single performance.)

Most of the artistes had already arrived including Colin Bower and his beautiful fiancée, Jill Edwards. We found

them a most charming couple. Colin made an admirable
compère and Jill helped too by drawing the winning lucky
programme number – the winner was not in the audience
so, although we were able to trace him, he missed having
his prize presented to him by such an attractive personality.

Also awaiting our arrival at the cinema was a message
from the U.S.A.F. base at Sculthorpe. Because of a measles
epidemic the children's choir would be unable to take part
in the show. This meant some quick rearranging as we
were left with only minutes before George Challice was
due to begin the opening music. And so that was why the
Electrons replaced the Blue Notes as our opening act.

With the tension back-stage nearing breaking-point, the
curtain rose, miraculously so it seemed, on time. The boys
got the show off to a lively start, they fully deserved the
enthusiastic response they received from the audience.

Two more acts followed, then it was my turn. I had
chosen a monologue with an appropriate religious theme,
"The Soldier's Bible". It tells the story of a serviceman
who is caught playing cards – or so it appears – during a
church service, and of how, at his court-martial, he explains
the Biblical association each card has for him.

Colin Bower filled in ably for the few minutes it took
to move me on to the stage and to adjust the height of the
microphone. At a prearranged signal Colin introduced me
and the curtain slowly parted.

All I could see was a very bright light shining from the
back of a huge black void. At the same time I was aware
that there were a large number of people out there somewhere. The school concerts at Ryburgh had been nothing
like this.

Without consciously realising it I had begun the monologue on cue, but suddenly I panicked. I knew I was going to forget the words. I could feel myself "drying up" completely as I hesitated slightly over each one. Then it was all gone and I felt perfectly calm again, the lines were once more crystal clear in my mind. I doubt whether my acute attack of nerves had lasted more than a minute or two but they were undoubtedly the worst moments of my life.

The remainder of the performance went smoothly. All too soon it was time for the entire cast to gather together on the stage for the final curtain. And what a wonderful reception the audience gave us. That and their immediate enquiries as to the date of the next show told us that all the work had been worthwhile.

To say that Susie and I believed that we had succeeded in producing a good show does not sound very modest. But in this case I feel we were justified in feeling that way, because of the not inconsiderable talents displayed by our fellow artistes.

The show was also a big financial success, our net profit was one hundred and twenty pounds. So in retrospect it seems ridiculous that our future activities never included another variety show. It is something that I always regretted, I still hope that it will be possible one day.

For the next three years we were one of the most active groups in Fakenham. As I was also kept busy with my studies during that period, life was rather chaotic at times. Although he never expressed his feelings in so many words, I believe there were times when Frank Lawson was afraid that my school-work would suffer as a consequence of my doing so much. His anxiety was unfounded however, as I always made sure that my studies came first.

I suppose the event that involved me with the most

work was the Inter-Organisations Quiz. It was a general knowledge contest run on a knock-out basis, in which we invited the town's numerous clubs and associations to take part. The preliminary rounds were held throughout the spring and summer months, then one evening in October during Aid the Disabled Week the finals took place.

I had the Herculean task of compiling over five thousand questions, the number required for each year's contest. With such a large number of questions it was not possible to double-check every one, this omission resulted in an awkward moment for me during a preliminary round.

A member of one team was an elderly vicar who had queried some of my answers on several occasions. But I foresaw no difficulties when, by pure coincidence, a religious question went to him on that particular evening. Imagine my consternation when his answer was different from the one I had written down. Firmly I told him that he was incorrect but naturally he was far from being convinced of this.

Immediately on arriving home I found that passage in the Bible – to my relief my answer was the correct one. Rather naughtily I wrote to the vicar giving the reference for that part of the text. In reply I received a most charming letter and from then on I found him much less argumentative. He got his revenge in the end though when he informed me with obvious delight that Magdalene College, Cambridge, is the same as "Maudlen".

The Club already marked Aid the Disabled Week with a church service and an autumn bazaar – we took over the responsibility for arranging the latter – when we added the Quiz finals to the week's events. We also introduced something to end the week, a dance.

During the dance – it was a Fancy Dress affair one year – we held a "Miss Happy Hearts" contest. The winning girl, chosen by a panel of judges, had certain duties to perform at Club functions throughout her year's reign. And very willingly those girls carried out their duties too.

In 1965 both Susie and I felt in need of a rest. Admittedly I found the work somewhat easier since I had ended my studies, but nevertheless we decided on a twelve month break as we were getting stale.

We could not have chosen a less auspicious time as Grace Wurr was leaving the district owing to her husband's retirement, and so the running of the Club was passing into fresh hands. We only learned of this after we had made our decision and so we abided by it, though I did compromise to a certain extent by serving for an extra year on the general committee.

As so often happens our intended rest period of one year extended into two years, then three and so on. Even though we have done nothing since October 1965, we still have constant requests from the public for another variety show or the return of the Inter-Organisations Quiz.

Susie has now resigned from the Club so if the Group was reformed it would have to be of a different format. Even so, I hope that sometime in the not too distant future something of the kind will be accomplished, because my association with the Group was a most enjoyable one.

13
Coming-of-Age

Now to return to my story at the point where I left it. If you recall, it was when I was awaiting the results of my G.C.E. exams at the end of 1963.

However, a few days before the results were announced I received an unexpected letter from the BBC. It informed me that the radio programme, "Have A Go", was visiting Fakenham early in January. If I wished to be considered for the programme I was to complete the enclosed questionnaire.

Presumably the BBC had contacted me because I had written to them the previous year requesting that Wilfred Pickles visit our district.

Apart from my parents and Bernard, I did not tell anyone about the letter. Although I completed the form I never expected to hear anything more about it. But I was mistaken as another letter arrived shortly afterwards instructing me to attend the Red Lion Hotel for an audition on the evening prior to the programme's transmission from Fakenham.

The evening of the audition was foggy but we arrived punctually at the hotel. We were shown into a large, first-floor sitting-room, where a number of people were already gathered.

While we waited refreshments were served. Then the producer conducted each contestant across the landing to a smaller room, where they were interviewed by Wilfred Pickles. Apart from Wilfred and Mabel – a typically, friendly Northern couple – the only other person present at the interview was a secretary. This nameless female appeared to make notes in shorthand of every word that was spoken.

My own interview lasted somewhat longer than most, because Wilfred was so interested in hearing all about the years I had spent in his native Yorkshire. At the end it was emphasised that the audition did not guarantee anyone a place in the programme, the six contestants would not be named until shortly before transmission began. Then, with the distribution of complimentary tickets, the audition came to an end.

The feeling of suppressed excitement in our house the following day was not wholly attributable to the possibility of my radio appearance. It was because the morning post had brought my exam results: I had passed in both subjects.

Our journey that evening to the new Secondary Modern School, from where the programme was being broadcast, was difficult as the fog was even more dense than it had been twenty-four hours earlier.

Even at that late stage there were only two more people who knew that I had auditioned for the programme. They were my Grandmother and Susie Peachment. Susie and I had been together at a club meeting that afternoon so it would have been odd if I had not mentioned anything to her. By not confiding in more people I would avoid all those embarrassing explanations if something went wrong.

Thirty minutes before transmission time, the producer stepped on to the stage to announce the names of the six contestants. The final name on his list was mine.

The lucky few then moved from their seats in the audience to the staff common-room, where Wilfred Pickles had a brief word with each one before we assembled on the stage. We sat in a line behind Wilfred and Mabel who were seated at a table in the centre of the stage. As it became the turn of each contestant they moved to an empty chair on Wilfred's left. The producer, wearing ear-phones, walked around continuously giving everyone their cue.

The broadcast went smoothly. But afterwards much of the enjoyment was spoiled for me by the hurtful attitude of two or three people, whom I had always regarded as friends. They were either cool in their manner towards me or completely ignored me. The experience taught me a great deal about human nature.

But I felt it had really been worthwhile, when a few days later I heard from Pam Turner, the school-girl pen-friend with whom I had lost touch some ten years ago. Through her mother hearing me on the radio Pam had succeeded in contacting me again, and this time we were both equally determined that our friendship would last.

I have found from personal experience that actually meeting a pen-friend can be a disappointment. This was certainly not the case, though, when we eventually visited Pam and her family at their new home in Chelmsford. They are such warm, friendly people, that from the very first meeting it was as if we had always known them. (We had to wait until their wedding day in 1966, before meeting Pam's fiancé, Brian Tapp.)

Once I had achieved my goal as regards my studies, I

was free to embark on my writing career. But first I decided to follow, or try to follow, some advice I had seen in an article directed at young writers. The article advised having an alternative career to rely on for financial security as it can be years, if ever, before an author makes a reasonable income from his work.

After giving the matter considerable thought I decided on taking an accountancy course, with a view to working from my home. Yet again I turned to Dr Lincoln Ralphs for advice.

My approach resulted in a comprehensive selection of literature on the subject being made available to me. Dr Ralphs promised me every assistance but he suggested that I study carefully the information supplied.

As I read the pamphlets it became clear that I would be unable to implement my plan, the main difficulty being that anyone embarking on such a course had to work in the office of a qualified accountant for a specified length of time. It was impossible for me to fulfil such a condition.

I next contacted our local welfare officer, and the special department of the employment exchange which deals with disabled workers.

The welfare officer did obtain some once a year work for me in the limited field of home typing. But as I was unable to cope with the toilet unaided, the employment exchange could not help in any way.

Our vicar at that time, the late Ronald Thompson, tried his utmost to persuade me to continue my scholastic studies. If it would have improved my chances of finding employment, then I would have been agreeable but as it was I felt that it would be pointless.

And so I began writing short stories with the intention of selling them to women's magazines. I think that at the beginning you believe that the editors are sitting in their offices waiting for just such a story as yours, so that first rejection slip can be shattering for the ego. After a while though one becomes used to the familiar bulky envelope in the post; yet another rejected manuscript. I always regretted that those attached slips of paper did not state precisely what was wrong with the story, and not simply that it was not suitable for their magazine.

The months and years passed by without success. But I found that more and more I was enjoying writing. I hoped too that the constant practice would improve my style.

But to return to 1964. As well as receiving my exam results that January and taking part in the "Have A Go" programme, it was also the year I celebrated my twenty-first birthday.

It was a wonderful day in which I seemed to do little else, other than open piles of cards and presents. It gave me a nice warm feeling to know that so many kind people had taken the trouble to send me their greetings. In the evening there was a large family party for me. When Bernard proposed my health he expressed a wish – that I wholeheartedly endorsed – that my second twenty-one years would be as successful as my first twenty-one had been.

It was in the summer of 1965 that Marilyn Gillies stayed at my home for a short holiday. This was partly due to the fact that the previous year Marilyn had flown to America to visit Mary Gordon, another armless person, with whom we had both been corresponding for about two years.

Mary, who was married with two perfectly normal sons, had sent both Marilyn and me much practical advice, it included detailed directions as to how she managed to dress herself. As it was rather difficult to visualise some of the manoeuvres involved, Marilyn believed that I would benefit – as she herself had done – from a practical demonstration.

We arranged to meet Marilyn at Peterborough, so I had my first glimpse of her as she walked with my mother out of the railway station there. She looked no different from the other passengers as her disability was disguised by the navy cape she was wearing. I had known that Marilyn was almost two years older than me, but she was also a foot taller. Her dark hair was short and wavy, and the dark frames of her spectacles swept upwards at the outer corners.

Naturally I had looked forward to Marilyn's visit but as the time for it had drawn nearer I had begun to feel absurdly nervous. I suppose it was because for the first time in my life I would be seeing myself as other people see me, having never personally encountered another armless person before then.

When the moment actually arrived, however, I found the experience strangely amusing. In particular I enjoyed seeing the expression on the faces of shop assistants when Marilyn "footed" money to them.

Marilyn, like Mary Gordon and myself, had this strange aversion to using artificial arms. It is difficult to explain why this is but I think it is because we believe, rightly or wrongly, that we can manage as well without them as we could with them. More recently I was watching a film on TV of Thalidomide children at play, and I noted with interest that although many of them were wearing artificial arms they were manipulating their toys with their feet.

One morning, as promised, Marilyn showed me how she

managed to dress herself. While standing on one leg she tossed the respective garment into the air with her other foot, then "headed" her way into it. By using two long-handled hooks Marilyn coped with the more intricate articles of apparel, as well as using them to operate zips to which she had attached large metal rings.

It was a lengthy operation as at that time Marilyn was still inexperienced and often several attempts had to be made before a garment was donned successfully. So, although my description is accurate, it does over-simplify things.

When I tried Marilyn's method sitting down, as I had to do, it simply did not work. The angle must have been wrong or something, at any rate the tossed garment just drifted away from me. But eventually I devised a method of my own.

For example, when putting on a dress I would fold the hem to the neck of the front of the dress. Tucking this under my chin I then crumpled the back of the garment between my teeth. By throwing my head backwards I could toss the back part over my head, after that it was only a matter of adjusting it with my foot. Removing it again was easy, as all I had to do was place the front part between my teeth, then toss it back over my head and so off.

Unfortunately I was never able to manage certain under-garments and so dressing myself was an unsuccessful endeavour. The increased activity enabled me to lose a little weight, but then after an illness some twelve months later I found the strain was too severe and so I had to abandon the project completely.

The trouble began on July 4th 1966, while I was on my Club's annual outing to Great Yarmouth. I was feeling no better when we returned to Fakenham and so we considered it wise for me to consult my own doctor before continuing my journey home to Gateley.

Since Dr Arthur's retirement the previous summer, my family's medical needs had been attended to by Dr John Nichols. Still comparatively young, this tall distinguished-looking man has a deep compassionate understanding for his fellow men. His constant kindness and genuine interest for his patients has made him a highly respected person.

Within a few minutes of my seeing Dr Nichols on the evening in question, he had confirmed my own diagnosis of a palpitation. He personally drove my mother and me home that evening, as he did not wish me to travel on the bus as originally planned.

Though rarely an indication of serious trouble, a palpitation can be extremely frightening. And, of course, the more tense one becomes, the worse the palpitation gets. It is something that one has got to learn to live with, difficult though that may be.

Only a short while before, Harold Cooke had made me a special drinking cup which I could use, even while lying flat on my back. This proved a godsend, as during the next few months I had to spend fairly frequent periods in bed.

At the same time Mr Cooke gave me an introduction to the late Bernard Newman, the author. I had found it becoming increasingly easy to be side-tracked from my aim to be a writer. Therefore, I was grateful for this introduction which encouraged me to begin again with renewed fervour.

14
Press, Radio and TV

The next two years passed by uneventfully but that does not mean that the days seemed long and dull, far from it. I have always found that you can find plenty to occupy your time with – if you really want to.

In the autumn of 1968, together with Susie Peachment, I was invited to address Red Cross personnel during one of their weekend conferences, to be held in Norwich. I had never taken part in that kind of thing before so it was with some reluctance that I accepted the invitation. However, the experience was quite painless and one that I rather enjoyed.

The theme of my speech was "How Voluntary Organisations Can Better Help the Disabled". I pulled no punches, I was determined to make the most of this rare opportunity to air my grievances. Amongst other points that I made, I emphasised the need for better wheelchairs, more social and working opportunities, in general a better deal for handicapped people. Probably one of the best ways such organisations can help us, is by putting pressure on the various Government departments to speed up these improvements.

My audience had taken notes whilst I had been speaking. As soon as I ended I was faced with a barrage of questions, particularly from the young cadets. I was greatly impressed by the deep understanding of the situation shown in the searching questions of those teenagers. I tried to give them as detailed answers as my limited time would allow.

The following January I was asked by my Club to represent them on Anglia TV's general knowledge quiz programme, "Try For Ten", which was visiting Fakenham. But unfortunately the producer would not accept me for the programme when he learned that I was confined to a wheelchair. So I had to wait a little longer to make my TV debut.

Although I could not take part in the programme, it was nevertheless an enjoyable evening. Not only was I able to have a chat with David Hamilton and Roz Early, the programme's compère and attractive red-haired hostess, but it was also most interesting seeing that type of programme being recorded. It is amazing how bright lights can turn pieces of coloured paper pasted on to cardboard, into that glamorous set we viewers see on our TV screens.

At this point I must return briefly to the subject of my health. Throughout 1969 I suffered from more frequent and more severe palpitations which I found both distressing and depressing, particularly as I had just come to terms with the trouble. And so Dr Nichols arranged for a heart specialist to visit me at my home on the morning of Sunday, October 19th.

This resulted in my being put on a course of a new drug which helps to control an erratic pacemaker. In my case this proved quite successful, as also the more modified type that I was changed to ten months later.

It was during my period of convalescence that there occurred one of those strange coincidences of life. It happened on October 29th, when I saw a report in our local

newspaper, the *Eastern Daily Press,* to the effect that
Marilyn Gillies had passed her driving test. I was delighted
about this as I knew it had been Marilyn's ambition ever
since she had seen Mary Gordon driving her specially
adapted motor car.

As well as sending Marilyn my congratulations, I wrote
to the editor of the paper explaining about my friendship
with Marilyn. That letter began a chain of events that
within a week had culminated in one of the most thrilling
moments of my life.

The next link in the chain was forged on Friday, October
31st. It took the form of a visit from the man who is now
assistant editor of the *Eastern Evening News,* Robert
Walker. At that time Mr Walker wrote a general interest
column for the morning paper, under the pseudonym of
Clement Court. And so his editor had suggested that a
follow-up to my letter might provide suitable material for
his column.

Mr Walker, a likeable middle-aged man, was easy to talk
to, he had learned well the art of interviewing. Once he had
gained our confidence a question was only used as a gentle
nudge to keep our words flowing freely. It was only when
she saw the interview in cold, hard print, that my mother
realised just how freely she had talked to Mr Walker.

The interview, sympathetically written, appeared in the
next morning's edition of the newspaper. I thought that
would be the end of the matter but it was not so, as I
learned early that same evening.

My family and I were finishing our tea when a red car
came to a stop outside our gate. Looking out into the gathering dusk, Bernard smilingly commented that it was Tony
Scase. (You will recall that it was Tony who interviewed me

for radio in 1962.) At first I thought that Bernard was joking, but then I realised that it really was Tony Scase.

Once again Tony was armed with a tape recorder because, following my write-up in the local press, he had come to interview me for the Monday edition of radio's "Regional Extra". Remembering that I had been chairman of my Club's Entertainment Group, Tony had thought that details of our current plans would make good subject matter for the interview. For a brief moment a look of consternation showed on his face as I quickly explained that the Group was no longer in existence, it looked for a while as if there would be nothing to interview me about, after all. However, during our general conversation I mentioned something which solved this dilemma.

Making new Christmas cards from used ones was another project started by Susie and me. It was a profitable scheme which the Club's committee agreed to continue with after the Entertainment Group had disbanded. And so, with Christmas less than two months away, it would be highly appropriate if I were to describe fully the method employed in making these cards. Which I did.

The whole affair reached its climax on the Monday. It was shortly before two o'clock that afternoon when I received another surprising visit from Tony Scase. His bosses had been so pleased with my broadcast that they wanted me to appear on BBC TV that evening, in the regional news programme, "Look East".

I was thrilled at this completely unexpected invitation but I hesitated over my reply. It was only fifteen days since the heart specialist had attended me at my home, and however much I wanted to appear on TV, I was not sure that it would be wise for me to do so. After some hasty deliberation on this point I agreed to take part in the programme, providing that Dr Nichols gave his consent.

Once he had extracted my promise Tony Scase returned to Norwich to make all the necessary arrangements, while my mother went to telephone the surgery. Dr Nichols was not there but the receptionist was able to contact him. Happily he gave his consent.

When I saw the doctor a few days later, I learned that he had been under the mistaken impression that the TV people were going to film me in my home. But whether this really influenced his decision or not, I do not know.

There was no time to tell any of my relatives or friends of this exciting development. Within two hours of my first knowing about it myself, dressed in my best outfit of champagne-coloured wild silk, I was with my mother in a taxi bound for Norwich.

Our friendly driver disclosed that he often drove for the BBC, so I suppose that he was well accustomed to keeping people's minds off the ordeal ahead. At any rate his incessant chatter was successful in keeping at bay any nerves that I might have had.

The evening dusk was deepening as we reached the studios, which from the outside resembled a large Victorian town house. We were greeted by Tony Scase, who led us into the building.

The "Look East" studio was a huge rectangular shaped room, which seemed to be overflowing with arc lights, cameras, and all the other paraphernalia of TV. At one end, seated behind a panel of soundproof glass, were the producer and his assistants.

On closer inspection I realised that the actual studio had been invisibly divided into four sections. Two of these were clearly intended for live interviews – it was obvious which corner was mine by the set which was decorated with the Christmas cards the BBC had bought from me – the remaining two sections were for the newsreader and the "link-man" who introduced each item in the programme.

The members of the production team were most kind and helpful. Having been told of my recent illness, they had arranged for me to go into the sound-proof gallery in between the times I was needed in the studio. This was a great relief to me, as I had been anxious as to how I would react to spending ninety minutes exposed to the intense heat coming from the bright lights.

The rehearsal was soon in progress. It began with the other studio interview, concerning a book written by two people who had been imprisoned by the Germans during the last war. Next came a film about boys canoeing, this was followed by a run-through of the day's news. Then it was my turn.

Everything went smoothly as Tony Scase had previously familiarised me with the questions he would be putting to me. (I imagine this is done to avoid any awkward pauses.)

There was just enough time for us to have a refreshing drink before assembling in the studio. I had always been under the impression that TV people never appeared in front of the cameras without wearing heavy make-up, but I was mistaken as none was worn that evening.

People who saw the programme remarked on the fact that I did not seem the least bit nervous. My worst moment came when the red light flashed on in the studio at the beginning of the programme, probably because I knew that it was then too late for me to change my mind. But I soon had myself firmly under control. After those first few moments the only thing that worried me was the heat, but the technicians kindly kept dimming those lights nearest me which was a great help. I think something of my discomfort must have shown on my face as Tony gave me some anxious looks. But by the time we reached my spot, the final item of the programme, I was feeling completely relaxed and beginning to enjoy myself.

As instructed, I tried to keep to my original words but even so the interview went faster than it had done at rehearsal. Despite Tony adding an impromptu question, the viewers had a longer look than usual at the weather card.

I know some people believed that I received at least twenty guineas for my TV appearance, which was ridiculous of course. In actual fact my fee was five guineas. (Apart from one exception, the only money I have earned so far in my life has been from the BBC.)

So one innocent letter to the editor of a newspaper had brought about my TV debut. I vowed after that to be wary of whom I wrote to in the future. And so I was, well for at least six months. That letter resulted in an event which I consider to be the final one worthy of mention here.

It was early in 1970 when I learned that Jimmy Savile was coming to East Dereham to open a boutique on Saturday, May 30th. Much as I would like to go, I knew that it would be unwise because of the crowds of people who would inevitably be there. And so, knowing of Jimmy's wonderful reputation regarding his charitable works, I sent him a letter explaining my difficulty and asking if it would be possible for him to come to my home.

To be honest I felt that it was only remotely possible that Jimmy would find time to fit my request into his schedule, particularly so as I received no reply to my letter. Nevertheless we hurried home that Saturday morning from doing our weekend shopping in Fakenham.

As we were sitting over an after lunch cup of tea, my mother commented on the unusual amount of police traffic, a motorbike and police car. We had momentarily forgotten about Jimmy, but when we saw that the police had come to a halt and that they were preceding two other cars, one an ancient Rolls-Royce, then we knew that our visitor could be none other.

Jimmy, dressed in a yellow ribbed cotton jersey suit with battledress jacket, was deeply tanned by the cruise he had returned from only a few short hours earlier. (That was the reason I had heard nothing from him.) He looks younger and more handsome than he appears on the TV screen, but otherwise just as I had imagined.

From the moment he came into the house Jimmy made himself at home. One of his opening remarks was "Put the kettle on, Ma." And he insisted that all ten members of his entourage, including three policemen and a chauffeur, join us for a cup of tea.

Jimmy's visit, which lasted half-an-hour, passed all too quickly. As he talked of his work in a Leeds hospital and of a little armless girl that he visits in Dublin, I caught brief glimpses of a serious and truly sincere man hidden beneath that zany humour. Jimmy had photographs taken with my family and taped an interview with me for his "Savile's Travels" radio programme.

After the departure of Jimmy's party, amidst kisses and waves, my mother announced that the excitement had been far too exhausting for her, she simply must sit down and have a nap. But we relived it all again as I recounted my story to a young newspaper reporter who called at my home later that afternoon.

I recollect thinking, as I drifted off to sleep that night, that even an isolated hamlet like Gateley has its day.

15
The Future?

At this point I would like to offer my patient reader a brief explanation as to how I came to write this book. That I have done so is mainly due to two men, Robert Walker and Dr John Nichols.

True, the idea did come first from members of my family but this was long before I thought seriously of becoming a writer. It was not until the matter was raised by Robert Walker in the late summer of 1969, that I gave it any real consideration. And then it was only after much deliberation that I finally took up my pen, the deciding factor being that Mr Walker had offered to read my work and advise me on it.

I had never found it easy to reveal my innermost feelings and thoughts, and I found it no easier to express them in the written word. So it was an extremely poor opening chapter that I sent to Mr Walker, rather like a bone with no meat on it.

Mr Walker's criticism was constructive. He made various comments on how my work could be improved without actually commenting on just how badly the chapter was written. At the end of his letter Mr Walker came to the crux of the matter, I needed to give more attention to detail. The fault was that I was not taking enough time over my work, something which would have to be rectified, I knew, if I was to have any success with the book.

Far from being spurred on to better efforts by Robert Walker's kind words, I abandoned the project completely, and began to plan the outline for a fictional story. But Fate decided to take a hand in the form of a visit from Dr Nichols.

Towards the end of his visit, Dr Nichols mentioned an article that he had read in the previous day's edition of the *Sunday Times*. It concerned an Irishman called Christy Brown.

Christy, who appears to be quite a character, has been severely disabled from birth because of brain damage. Though still unable to speak with much clarity, Christy has learned through the years to use his left foot, the only limb in which he has controlled movement. This has enabled him to communicate more fully with his fellow human beings and to prove that far from being the cabbage he was once thought to be, he does in fact possess a remarkable intelligence.

I learned much of this from Dr Nichols who also told me that Christy Brown had written his life-story. It seemed rather as if I were surrounded by a band of conspirators when the doctor added, "That's something that you should do. You could you know."

We all have some purpose in life and after that I began to wonder if I was being shown that mine was to write this book after all. I felt, too, that I ought to do something to justify the faith other people seemed to have in my writing ability. So after yet more heart-searching, I put the last remnants of my reluctance behind me and dusting off my manuscript I began again. And this time I took the precaution of consulting my former tutor, Frank Lawson, before showing any of those early chapters, now considerably altered, to Mr Walker.

Once they knew of my renewed effort, Bob Walker and Dr Nichols, each in their separate way, endeavoured to keep me from any further back-sliding with their enquiries as to how the book was progressing. But they need not have feared as I was now equally determined to see my book completed. Nevertheless, I found their constant interest most encouraging.

Now that I am at last in sight of my objective I can allow myself a little time to think about the future. I am not a particularly ambitious person but I do have two ambitions that I would like to fulfil. The first of these is to make a successful career for myself in the world of fiction writing. Secondly – in a more lighthearted vein – I hope one day to attend a football match at Old Trafford, the home ground of Manchester United.

Whether or not I shall realise either of these ambitions remains uncertain. What I do know is that the future holds no fears for me. I realise however that there will always be problems for me to face, especially when I no longer have my parents. But it would be pointless for me to waste my life worrying over this. I believe that the pattern of our lives is determined before we are born, I suppose it is this philosophy that enables me to accept so calmly whatever life holds.

Probably, as you have read this book, you have formed some idea of the kind of person that I am. I wonder how your impressions compare with the following self-analysis.

Basically I am a happy person with an almost impish sense of humour, but beneath this lighthearted exterior there lurks a more serious side to my nature, one rarely seen by others. I like having people around me yet I am not bored with my own company. If I am really interested in something then I tackle it with energetic determination, otherwise I can be almost lazy in my approach to work. I am never happier than when I am called upon to use my organising ability – I must have a bossy streak somewhere.

Though I have an affectionate nature I am slow to give deep affection, but once I do give it then it is lasting. My love of animals and children is mutual.

I loath any form of deception. If I suspect that things are not as above-board as they should be, then I am like a dog worrying a bone until I have discovered the truth of the matter. This trait has at times made me most unpopular in certain quarters, as also has my habit of speaking my mind. But I believe strongly in fairness and honesty at all times.

I cannot recall when it was that I first began making jocular remarks about my disability whenever a suitable opportunity arose. Over the years it has become such a habit that I have to keep a careful watch on my tongue when strangers are present, I would never intentionally embarrass, or hurt, anyone.

Nor was there a time in my life when I was suddenly aware of being different from anyone else. Some people mistakenly believe that a disabled person is conscious of this every waking moment of their life. Were this true, life would be intolerable.

If one has to be disabled then I feel that it is best to have been afflicted since birth. With the need to change your way of life (which inevitably follows a disabling accident or disease) eliminated, the experience is much less traumatic. But whatever the circumstances, one has to come to terms with a disability – the sooner the better for all concerned – and then as far as is practicable, ignore it.

My unquestioning acceptance of my own situation was probably due to a large extent to the commonsense approach of my family. Their successful determination to treat me as a normal person not only influenced my own attitude but, in turn, that of other people. So much so, that both acquaintances and close friends have commented on a number of occasions that even when they are in my company they are frequently totally unaware of my disability. To me, this is one of the greatest compliments I could receive.

In recent years there have been considerable improvements made as regards aid for the handicapped section of the community. But as yet we are only seeing the tip of the iceberg, there is still a long way to go.

There is an urgent need for better-designed and more comfortable wheelchairs, for many of us spend two-thirds of our life sitting in them. And then again, there must be greater understanding of our needs, and of our insistence to be treated normally.

But at least the growing enlightenment in the attitude of ablebodied people means that, whether their disability be mental or physical in its origin, there is no longer the need for the severely handicapped to remain within the close confines of their homes. With our increasing advent on the streets, the general public have grown accustomed to the sight, or maybe they are in too great a hurry these days, but whatever the reason they do not turn around for that second look as often as they used to do.

I can well recall the day one of these dear ladies walked into a lamp standard and was told by my brother, "It serves you right. Perhaps you will look where you are going in future."

These kind of incidents never troubled me in the least, I simply put it down to ignorance and found it rather amusing. But I doubt if my family dismissed them so lightly.

However, there are two groups of people that do annoy me. There are those, of whom I have had personal experience, who treat the physically handicapped as children and rather backward ones at that. And then there are the kind who treat the prospect of our having a serious emotional relationship with a member of the opposite sex, as something to be laughed at or as something disgusting which has to be crushed at all costs.

I suppose the biggest upheaval of my life came when I left home to go to boarding school. I was fortunate however, as Welburn was a happy school and I enjoyed every moment that I was there.

Without a doubt these special schools do a magnificent job, the handicapped child has so few chances to learn independence. Yet the environment is somewhat sheltered and does not prepare one for the outside world where they have to compete with the ablebodied. So whenever practicable I think it is an excellent idea for a handicapped child to attend a normal school, even if only for a short while.

I was saddened recently to learn of the premature death of Hywel Williams, coming as it did only a few short months after his retirement from the headmastership of Welburn Hall Special School. He was, in my opinion, one of the few people who have a deep understanding of the needs of the disabled. Above all else, Mr Williams respected the wishes of the handicapped children under his care to be treated as normal human beings. I shall remember him always with great affection.

I have only one regret, the time I spent in a Leeds hospital. It is easy to be wise after the event but I could have put those wasted years to such good use. Yet life has its compensations, I formed some truly lasting friendships during that time.

In retrospect I consider that I have been very lucky. I have been blessed with a devoted family, many wonderful friends and a good brain. What more could I have asked for?

I should like to think that by telling my story I have given encouragement and hope to some of my fellow disabled. If I have succeeded in this then I am more than pleased. But I have, I hope, left no doubts in my reader's mind that life in a wheelchair can be great fun.

Afterword

by Mr Jimmy Savile O.B.E.

So I called to see Mo and it did cross my mind to kidnap her. When she slapped my face with her foot I realised she could give me big troubles, like all dolly birds.

Cancelling the kidnap idea we all settled down for tea, page 117, and I left having found a new girl-friend.

Her book must sell well otherwise she cannot keep me to the style of which I'm used. Otherwise I'll just have to send her out to work!